Early Spelling

Early Spelling takes an entirely new look at the phenomena of spelling. It sets the subject in a wider context than any existing study has done so far. Its constant aim is to reveal children's spelling as a resource for a rich and varied set of meanings. In a period in which literacy is a newly intense concern, and in which questions around skills, competence, authority and innovation are seen as central in debates around the shapes of education, its curricula and its purposes, spelling assumes a particularly charged relevance.

Gunther Kress shows how looking at a child's spelling can help us to understand the child's engagement with the world. Tensions between the demands of authority and convention and the dynamics of creativity and innovation are reflected in the child's writing and spelling. These issues are explored through analysis of the many meanings of spelling, what children try to spell, and the look and sound of spelling.

Early Spelling is illustrated throughout with examples of spelling and drawing by children aged from 18 months to 12 years old. **Gunther Kress**'s commentaries on these address how we might come to understand children and their view of the world, and how we understand language in its written form. This original approach to fundamental questions within a clear and accessible format will appeal to students, academics and professionals involved in the issues of literacy at any level.

Gunther Kress is Professor of English/Education at the Institute of Education, University of London. His previous publications include *Learning to Write* and *Before Writing*, both published by Routledge.

Early Spelling

Between convention and creativity

Gunther Kress

London and New York

First published 2000 by Routledge
11 New Fetter Lane, London EC4P 4EE

Simultaneously published in the USA and Canada
by Routledge
29 West 35th Street, New York, NY 10001

Routledge is an imprint of the Taylor & Francis Group

© 2000 Gunther Kress

Typeset in Baskerville by J&L Composition Ltd, Filey, North Yorkshire
Printed and bound in Great Britain by Biddles Ltd, Guildford and Kings
Lynn

British Library Cataloguing in Publication Data
A catalogue record for this book is available from the British Library

Library of Congress Cataloging in Publication Data
Kress, Gunther R.
    Early spelling: between convention and creativity / Gunther Kress.
        p.   cm.
    Includes bibliographical references (p.) and index.
    ISBN 0–415–18065–1 (hbk.).   ISBN 0–415–18066–X (pbk.)
    1. Language and languages – Orthography and spelling. 2. Children –
Language. 3. Literacy. 4. Creativity (Linguistics) I. Title.
P240.2.K74 1999   99–24810
401'.93–dc21   CIP

ISBN 0–415–18065–1 (hbk)
ISBN 0–415–18066–X (pbk)

For Jill

Contents

Preface

As we enter the new century and the new millennium, education is dominantly there on the public agenda – and rightly so. Are we anxious about this new world? Are we uncertain about its shape? Yes, utterly. Are we clear how to encounter this era of uncertainty? Are we clear how to deal with our anxiety? No, absolutely not. These questions provide the context in which this book is written; and they (nearly) define my purposes for writing it now.

This may seem an odd way to preface a book of this kind, with one foot in education, and the other in the study of language broadly seen. But language has, throughout the history of human kind, furnished potent metaphors for social and political life, and spelling is, in this regard, the quintessence of language. Metaphors – and real practices – around freedom or control, conformity and convention or freedom and creativity are easily and quickly developed around spelling. If the period from the mid-1960s to the late 1970s had seen a near total relaxation around the teaching of spelling, then the present is witnessing an extraordinary political concern with the reimposition of such rules. What is going on?

All of us are reduced to speculating – to guessing about our future. No one can be certain how best to prepare for it. This is where opinions divide. One suggested path is a return to practices that seemed to serve in the past; another path, much talked about, much advertised, much advocated even, but not implemented anywhere, is an attempt to gain some sense of the shape of the future and to find the means *now* to prepare for it.

So what can we know about this future, from our position in the post-industrial societies of the 'West'? We know that mass production of the nineteenth-century form has gone. Mass institutions of that era – mass society with its class structures, with mass armies, mass bureaucracies, mass media, mass markets, the mass institutions of the hospitals, schools, railways – have all disappeared, are disappearing, or are coming under the severest challenge. In their place new forms are appearing, far less stable, far less long-lived; lifestyle groupings, constantly shifting in their constitutions; new forms of media; new forms of economic activity; and so on. It is now accepted as a truth that in this future no one will keep a job for a lifetime. In the United States the average period that employees from middle managers upwards spend in any one company is now four years.

Flexibility is the new keyword. A flexible labour force is what is required by all: that too is part of the new commonsense. This flexible labour force ('Eager to stay; happy to go' is the motto for the ideal member of the new learning corporation with its flattened hierarchy, and its distributed knowledge) is expected to have other characteristics: adaptability of course, but also being innovative, creative, positive in relation to constant change. No doubt some, perhaps a lot, of this new commonsense is facile, ideological and extremely short-term thinking. What is not in doubt is that the complex changes that have brought us 'globalization' have brought conditions that are here to stay for a long time, and certainly well into the twenty-first century. This complex contains factors that will continue to unmake past arrangements and to abolish existing social, cultural, economic framings; and these factors rule out an early arrival at new stabilities, at the new global, (more) local and intermediary levels. I am thinking here of globalization of finance, of culture, of the enormous speeding up of transport, the shifts of information as the basis of new industries and of the economy overall.

Education, in its nineteenth-century guise, had as its aim to meet the needs of its society. For a century and a half these needs stayed relatively stable, so that the forms and structures of education could also remain relatively stable. It seemed, in that context, as though the task of education was to reproduce the culture by making the young grow up in the image of the former generation. That is not a possibility now. Even the shorter-term future looks a lot different from the immediate past. An economy that has changed from the dominance of industrial mass production to the dominance of information industries (and to a lesser extent of service industries) cannot be sustained effectively by the contents, structures, values, and processes of an education system that had developed to serve an entirely different economy.

If human dispositions towards stability, reliable replication and competent reproduction were essential in the past, then these are not the essential requirements for the new economy. It demands – even now – dispositions towards innovativeness, creativity, the challenge of the established, the existent. The fundamental question for education – if it is still to serve its society well – is: How can this be done? What changes in curricula will there need to be? What changes in pedagogic practices? What changes in values, contents, ethics?

Spelling seems a truly slight point to apply the lever of Archimedes for the rethinking and remaking of that vast complex. And yet perhaps it is not so slight: language, as I said, has always served as a potent metaphor for social values, structures and practices. Spelling is that bit of linguistic practice where issues of authority, of control, of conformity can be most sharply focused. Spelling is the domain par excellence – no matter how tiny it may seem – where the politics of conformity can be sheeted home. It is equally a place where, with a different set of priorities and different understandings, we might be able to see the inherent creativity, the innovativeness of young humans, right at the centre of the space that seems absolutely dominated by convention.

This defines (nearly) my purpose in writing this book. Unless we come to understand – really, truly, profoundly – that humans are creative even in a domain where convention, conformity and control seem to rule absolutely, unless we come to understand that as a fact, then we cannot hope to remake education so that it may serve the essential needs of the new economic and social environments.

In the UK, as in many anglophone countries around the world, the politics of conformity are coming to dominate education, even at the very time when politicians tell us that the challenges of the new world can only be met through adaptability, through innovativeness. The indicators of achievement are set more narrowly, more tightly, more for the short term. This is hugely ironic, in many ways: in the age that declares itself as superindividualist, conformity of individual performance to narrower goals is beginning to dominate education, from the university to the kindergarten. If this continues unabated, it will prove disastrous for the productive capacities – cultural, economic, ethical, and social – of the societies that have allowed themselves to be taken along that path. As a society we have begun to take the route of turning knowledge into information – which is an essential move – without at the same time caring for the continued production of new knowledge. But if you decide to eat the seedcorn of intellectual production, then you will face intellectual starvation after the next harvest.

It seems clear to all commentators that what is needed is a culture of innovation: this will be the most prized and most essential commodity in the era of the new economies. Levels of economic activity are directly linked to this. All available indicators suggest that the UK (as one instance) lags behind most post-industrial societies on this dimension. But this culture of innovation will have to include everyone – right down to the service worker. That defines the task for education.

In this context I want to ask some other questions. I regard them as essential if we want to consider choosing and travelling on the other paths. What is the world of our children likely to be like? In what ways have the life-worlds of school and work, of school and leisure/pleasure, of in-school and out-of-school, begun to diverge? How do children see the world? What do they think it is like? What are the real capabilities and capacities of our children, and how could we hope to find out? How could they be harnessed to the new demands of this future world?

These questions define the other part of my purpose. I do not wish to produce something that is merely a piece of rhetoric. That would serve no one; that would be worse than what we have. In the end, my interest remains that of the traditional academic project: I want to know what the world that I am concerned with is actually like. What are the truths that I can hope to discern and establish? I am, to put it simply, interested in understanding what children do, how they act in the world: to know, perhaps, how they see the world; to know how they think. This fits with my first purpose, because I want to apply that insight, that knowledge, in order to effect essential changes in educational thinking as much as in educational practices. In the area of my own competence, educational thinking and educational practice do need to change. The questions – what are the new demands posed by that future world? what specific knowledge, what precise skills, what dispositions will be needed to meet them adequately? – have hardly begun to be put, let alone answered. These are real demands, that institutional education must meet, or become irrelevant.

However, to do this requires the courage to take a new look: or perhaps not all that new – others, as I indicate in the bibliography, have gone a part of that way already. My new look proceeds from a simple standpoint: human (cultural) actions are always meaningful, and that includes the actions of children. Spelling is a cultural action: therefore all aspects of spelling are meaningful. Spelling represents a set of resources that is used to make meaning. I want to find out what these meanings are, where they point, and how 'the new' comes about in that context. That is the position from which I reconsider children's early spelling: a system seemingly entirely subject to the constraints of convention, and yet one that children (and adults too) make into the site of creativity.

I do not advocate that children should not be taught, and should not learn, to spell. That would be entirely unjustifiable while social pressure places so much weight on conformity in this practice. At the same time it is worth reminding ourselves that we already live in the age of the spell-checker, that makes it difficult for me to use spellings that diverge from the word-processing programs of my machine. My aim is to uncover children's dispositions, to learn to understand their energetic efforts to represent their world accurately from their perspective, and in that process to gain better understandings of them and of their ways of thinking. That understanding will be the foundation for devising the curricula that will allow education fully to serve its old and proper purposes: namely those of sustaining a productive society.

It may be helpful to say a word on the examples on which this book is based. In the main they consist of materials that I have collected in a relatively unsystematic way: things written at home, in school, by our two children, by their friends, and some examples from further afield – writing that was usually a part of some other complex activity, very often games of some kind, games of shops or banks, of school, or of other imagined activities. At times writing was central, in schoolbooks, for instance, or on cards or letters. I lay no claim to representativeness. My aim is to extend the scope within which spelling needs to be considered: to expand the scope of the notion of spelling itself, to put consideration of spelling into an essential wider environment. I hope that my account can provide new ways of considering this phenomenon, and that these might feed into practices of teaching in the widest way.

I hope that I have been able to do some justice to, and to capture even if in some slight way, the acuity, the seriousness, the sheer intelligence and the care – the intense concern to get it right – that suffuses the writing and making of the young people represented here. My thanks go to them first and foremost: to Michael Kress and Emily Kress, to their friends, and to the other young spellers not personally known to me whose work appears here. The ideas that I brought to these materials come from many years of working with and learning from many people: most recently perhaps particularly in my collaboration with Theo van Leeuwen, Carey Jewitt, Mary Scott, Anton Franks, Jon Ogborn, Jim Gee, Mary Kalantzis, Bill Cope, Pippa Stein, Denise Newfield and Brian Street. I owe real thanks to the reviewers of the initial proposal and of early drafts for their perceptive and helpful comments: two whose names I know are Roz Ivanič and David Barton. I have been fortunate to work in an intellectually productive environment at the Institute of Education in the University of London. It is a place where educational professionals from around the globe work and learn, and I have benefited enormously from working and learning with them. I owe particular thanks to three of them, who allowed me to use some of their materials: Kwok Kam Fun, Tsai Hu-Sun, and Kate Pahl. My immediate intellectual home – the Academic Group, Culture Communication and Societies – has provided me with a rich set of contrasting and complementary ideas and traditions in a productive collegial environment.

This book has been written in the ever fewer and smaller interstices of academic life. In this I have had the constant help and support, in so many different ways, of Judy Demaine: without her help I would not be writing these last few sentences now. My sincere thanks go to Louisa Semlyen and to Miranda Filbee at Routledge for patience and encouragement, dispensed in equally generous measure, and to Jody Ball for her great care in the production stages of the book. Professional lives and personal lives touch everywhere, and without Jill none of this would have happened in any case.

Sources and context

The question of spelling is back on the political and educational agenda with a fierce insistence. But the question of the spelling of English, of children's engagement with the problems of English orthography, has a history of a truly venerable age. In a section of this book I put a particular starting point, broadly the turn from the sixteenth to the seventeenth century, when that became an issue – in many different ways – for English grammarians. Since then this has been a continuous concern, sometimes strongly, sometimes waning. A renewed and more recent impetus was given by the work of English scholars, at the end of the nineteenth and the beginning of the twentieth century, attempting to describe the sound system of English (portrayed or caricatured in George Bernard Shaw's figure of Professor Higgins in *Pygmalion*). A.C. Gimson's book *An Introduction to the Pronunciation of English* (1962) stands in that tradition.

The ready availability of the reel-to-reel tape-recorder in the 1950s made possible a much more intense study of language-as-speech than had ever been possible before, and **speech** as distinct from **writing** began to be a focus of research – not just speech-as-sounds but speech-as-text. This gave new flavour to the study of spelling, because now the problems could be seen not just as a matter of the relation of discrete sounds (in the immediate environment of adjacent sounds) to individual letters (or combination of letters), but as a matter of quite wide environments, in which grammatical, syntactic and textual factors could be seen to play a part. Academic work on spelling now proceeds on a number of fronts: still with the focus on the minute details of sounds, in the context of syllables for instance (here the work of Goswami and Bryant (1990) is particularly relevant), but also, since the 1970s, with an increasing focus on a much wider environment, in the work of Nigel Hall (1987; 1992) for instance, and of Ken and Yetta Goodman, in what came to be known as the real language movement. In his recent *Fonic Fallacies* Ken Goodman (1996) mounts a strong argument against approaches whose frames of relevance are implausibly narrow. In many ways, even if in a quite different vein, my arguments put forward in this book belong in the tradition of taking a very wide environment as an essential frame of reference for understanding spelling.

Views of language will always have an immediate effect on ideas about spelling, and views of language are, in our period, in the process of a deep, fundamental change towards a conception of language that is much more social, and yet is connected everywhere with the psychological and cognitive dimensions of human beings. The work of the Russian psychologist L.S.Vygotsky (1978; 1986) has been enormously influential here both directly, and in the work of neo-Vygotskians such as Wertsch (1991). The interest in Vygotsky coincides with a broader interest in the social, political and ideological dimensions of language (where Soviet Russian psychological, linguistic and literary theoretical work, and Marxist theory in general, has also been deeply important). The recent book *The Politics of Writing* by Romy Clark and Roz Ivanič (1997) is a strong representative in that tradition; Chapter 8 in their book, 'Issues of correctness and standardisation in writing,' bears directly on many issues in the present book. There is a developing strand in theorizing in linguistic work that forges a close integration of social factors and linguistic form. Norman Fairclough's *Language and Power* (1989) is an accessible source for this work, and the links with thought (cognition) are strongly made in Jim Gee's work, overtly so in his *The Social Mind* (1992; see also 1990). Gee also makes a powerfully convincing case for the link of thought, language, education and the economy.

Class, history and language impinge everywhere on spelling. In this book I make a brief reference to Schonell's reading tests, in which a thousand years of the history of English society, transformed into the history of the English language, appear as a present effect in a still class-divided educational system through what David Corson (1985) calls 'the lexical bar'. The Norman Conquest and its social and linguistic consequences are still with us. But contemporary Western societies are now in the midst of social, cultural and linguistic transformations of an extent that may turn out to be as significant as the great population changes in Europe at the end of the Roman Empire, events that brought forms of a Germanic language to England, to be overlaid (in a period of some 500 years) by forms of a Romance language (first Norman and then Angevin French). Dick Leith's book (1983) on the history of the English language gives a wonderful account of that, but Ben Rampton's and Mark Sebba's books – *Crossings* (1996), and *London Jamaican* (1994) – bring us right into the present, and show us what vast, fast changes are happening with(in) English right now, in the pluricultural sites of urban Britain.

Settled notions of spelling simply cannot stand up to the actuality, the speed of the changes that are happening before our eyes, and as evidence – if we wish to take notice – for our ears. This is transformation, this is creativity; it is tangible evidence that humans are always transformative and creative – even if in some periods this is overlooked, suppressed or denied. Early spelling as creative act has also been commented on for a considerable time now: in the work of Charles Read (1986), as in that of Ann Haas-Dyson, and of Glenda Bissex (1980), who document this with great clarity and persuasiveness; Kamler and Killorr (1983) is work in the same vein. Of course, having something shown is no guarantee of 'absorbing' and acting on such information. This is why I attempt to bring the issue to the fore again: yes, we have 'known' that children's spellings are creative, that the minds of children are constantly actively at work in re-making, re-inter-preting, and re-shaping their world – and here the work of Jerome Bruner (1990; 1996) is full of insights – and yet, in the contemporary public common sense, this has not become knowledge in the sense of 'fully understood and actively used' knowledge.

There is, in one sense, nothing that is new in this book – not in the areas just described, nor in another area, which says 'language is, among other things, a visual phenomenon. Writing is a form of image.' Myra Barrs' article 'Maps of play' (1988) makes that point, and Vygotsky certainly drew attention strongly to this fact. Oliver Sacks' extraordinarily challenging book *Seeing Voices* (1991) shows us in just how many ways and through how many sensory means we make mean-ing. In a similar vein, though with different intellectual origins, is the work of Howard Gardner, whose *Frames of Mind* (1993) establishes a powerful case for the multiplicity and diverseness of thinking – of cognition – and the relation of think-ing to different forms of receiving information through the senses. All this under-mines any notion of thought being equatable with language, and of rationality depending on language – or of spelling being merely a neutral translating exer-cise, rather than creative and productive. It also undermines any notion of lit-eracy-as-meaning or of meaning-as-literacy beginning with formal school-based writing. The notion of literacy as embedded in hugely diverse practices – and emerging from these – has long been recognized. The work of Sulzby stands in that tradition, giving rise to an understanding of literacy as gradually 'emerging' over a long period of the child's engagement in her or his social and cultural world. In a somewhat different yet deeply related way so does the work of Barton and Hamilton, whose *Local Literacies* (1997) traces the diverseness, the social, prac-tical embeddedness of literacy in the everyday, everywhere embedded in the micro-histories of everyday life.

Where my own thinking may be distinctive is in two issues perhaps: that mean-ing is made in many different ways, and that the outwardly made signs (whether as spelling, as novel, as gesture, or as 3D object) always manifest the interests of their makers. The first of these is outlined in books such as *Social Semiotics*, or *Reading Images*; the second is overtly there in books such as the two mentioned, as in *Learning to Write*, and *Before Writing: Rethinking the Paths to Literacy*. The conse-quences of these two points **taken seriously** are, I believe, profound: they force us to search for meaning in all social acts of humans large or small, and they force us always to treat all such acts as multiply meaningful. Spelling as a consequence becomes a hugely complex process of making meaning. This work stands in close relation to much other recent work. For instance, David Olson's *The World on Paper* (1994), Kate Pahl's *Transformations: Meaning Making in Nursery Education* (1999), and the work of Sacks (1991), Gardner (1993), Gee (1990; 1992), and van Leeuwen (1999). In the end, 'making' is always social, and it is always the work of very many people, whether that is visible or not. That applies to the making of the ideas in this book.

List of phonetic symbols used in the book

The dialect assumed in these instances is that of a middle-class, well-educated speaker of Standard English, broadly from south eastern England.

Vowels

/ɪ/	as in	bit
/iː/		heat
/u/		put
/uː/		food
/e/		bed
/o/		pot
/oː/		sword
/æ/		bad
/a/		bath
/ʌ/		hut
/ə/		any unstressed vowel, e.g. as in butt**er**

Semi-vowels

/j/	as in	yacht
/w/		which

Diphthongs

/ei/	as in	pain
/ai/		time
/oi/		toy
/au/		cow
/əu/		home

Consonants

/t/	as in	ten
/d/		den
/p/		pin
/b/		bin
/g/		go
/m/		meat
/n/		neat
/r/		red
/l/		lead
/f/		fed
/v/		hover
/ʃ/		shoot
/ʒ/		binge
/s/		so
/z/		zoo
/ng/		sing
/θ/		thin
/ð/		then
/h/		hunger

Introduction

0.1 So what *is* spelling?

We all know what spelling is. Spelling is knowing how to write words correctly. But if that is what it is, why are there so many rules that seem to tell us how to relate the sound of a word in spoken language to the look of a word in written language? If spelling is simply a matter of reproducing, correctly, the remembered sequence of letters that make a written word, then all the stuff about the relation to the **sound** of language is quite beside the point. Or, perhaps, it is a marginal and quite separate matter, a question of having **rules for sounding written language**.

The first approach is more or less the decision seemingly implied in the German word *Rechtschreiben* – 'writing (it) right': getting all the letters correct; and certainly nothing about fussing with the sound.

In the English word *spelling*, however, quite a lot of the sense of **transcribing** from one mode of communication (speech) to another (writing) remains. In English we seem to be stuck with a typical compromise: yes, spelling is a matter of the **look** of words; yes, there is **visual spelling**; and yes, spelling is a matter of the relation of speech and writing, a question of getting the right letter sequences to capture the sound of the language. The rules of spelling promise to provide a reliable means of getting from the sound of language to the look of language in terms of sequences of letter shapes. This ignores an uncomfortable fact, however: the rules of spelling do not start from sound and guide you to writing; rather, they start from writing, and guide you (should you wish to be guided in that direction) to the pronunciation of letter sequences in sound. So we have a compromise that is more flawed than compromises ought to be.

But at least we might say, spelling is about rules of recording: either the recording in graphic form of remembered word shapes as letter sequences, or the recording of heard sound sequences into uncomfortably fitting letter-shape sequences. Spelling is either putting in letter form what I have had stored in my brain – in my memory – or it is the translation from the medium of sound into the medium of graphic substance (letters). The first of these approaches is straightforward. In it, spelling is putting words-as-images on some surface, through the medium of letters. The graphic image of the written word *cat* exists in my brain as *cat*; and I know that it corresponds to a sound sequence such as /kæt/. The second of these approaches is more troublesome. If spelling is the transduction, the recording in letters of the sounds of speech, then the problem arises that no spelling ever transcribes or records more than a fraction of that sound. Who makes, or who has made, the decision as to what should be recorded and what should not? For instance, if you say *cat*, then you'll notice an *h*-like sound after the initial /k/: but that isn't ever written down. Similarly at the end of the word: if you say the word carefully, you'll hear a similar sound as part of the /t/; the sounds written down should be /khæth/ or even /khæts/, with a slight /s/ at the end.

The explanation for all this is that we have a notion of what an idealized /k/ or /t/ is, and we are happy to ignore the fact that the ideal never exists. And perhaps that's fair enough. But we now admit that spelling is about an abstraction: an abstracted set of sounds related to sequences of letters. However, there are many more problems where this came from. For instance, words are always integrated into a chain of speech: they have a context. So I'm likely to have said 'No, that wasn't my cat that killed your budgie', with a high intonation on *my* falling right away down to *cat*. The item /kæt/, in other words, is not just a sequence of speech sounds, but is said with an intonational contour that is part of the meaning of that utterance. That meaning, that aspect of sound, is not recorded either.

Some things, it seems, are not spelled – even though they are highly meaningful. Spelling, in English, is only ever a partial recording of what goes on in sound; and if spelling is about recording meaning, then it only ever records a part of the rich meanings of an utterance. Most aspects of the sound of language are never spelled at all.

Now the idea that spelling is about meaning may seem quite fanciful: yes, of course, the things that **are** spelled have meaning, but surely, the spelling itself does not? But consider the – admittedly unusual – spelling of an 8-year-old from Hong Kong shown in Figure 0.1.

The child's first language has a pictographic writing system: the so-called 'characters' of Chinese. Here the child is learning not just a new language, English, but also a new transcriptional system, the Roman version of the alphabet. In his 'own' system the relation between writing system and 'language' is very roughly one where (complex) characters represent ideas. So, when this child learns English, he has to learn not only another language, but also a completely different conception of what the writing system is and does. In an alphabetic system the symbols represent (roughly speaking) sounds. At a second step, ideas can get attached to sequence of sounds.

So, to contrast:

in the pictographic script	**in the alphabetic script**
Step 1: symbols (characters) stand for ideas	symbols (letters) stand for sounds
Step 2: symbols (characters) can have the sounds of speech attached to them	symbols (letters) can have ideas/concepts attached to them

What is spelled in Chinese is ideas/concepts; what is spelled in English is sounds. In Chinese the ideas/concepts can have sounds attached to them; in English the sounds can have ideas attached to them. At a first level, the question 'what is writing, and what is language?' would be answered differently in Chinese and English.

What is writing?	In Chinese	In English
	writing is the spelling of ideas by conventionalized images (characters)	writing is the spelling of sounds by conventionalized images (letters)

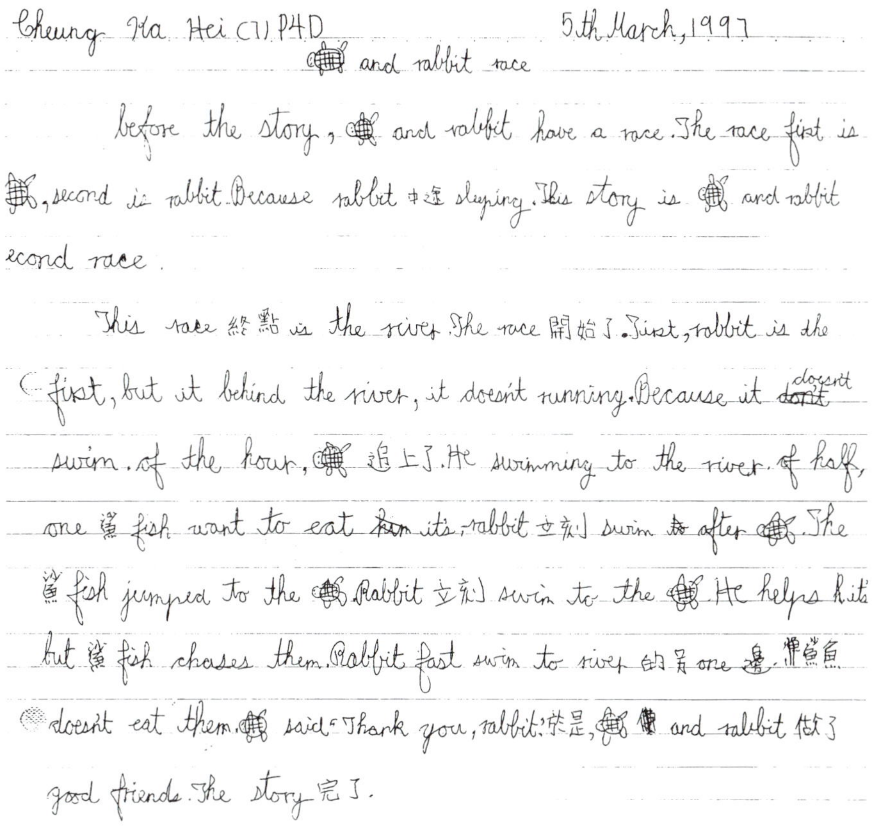

Cheung Ka Hei (1) P4D   5th March, 1997

🐢 and rabbit race

before the story, 🐢 and rabbit have a race. The race first is 🐢, second is rabbit. Because rabbit 在 sleeping. This story is 🐢 and rabbit second race.

This race 終點 is the river. The race 開始了. First, rabbit is the first, but it behind the river, it doesn't running. Because it doesn't swim. of the hour, 🐢 追上了. He swimming to the river of half, one 鯊 fish want to eat him it's rabbit 立刻 swim to after 🐢. The 鯊 fish jumped to the 🐢. Rabbit 立刻 swim to the 🐢. He helps him but 鯊 fish chases them. Rabbit fast swim to river 的另 one 邊. 鯨鯊魚 doesn't eat them. 🐢 said "Thank you, rabbit." 於是, 🐢 🐇 and rabbit 做了 good friends. The story 完了.

Figure 0.1 Hare and tortoise

The point of this is to show that spelling is always the spelling of something, and probably in all cases – even in English (if less visibly so) – it is the spelling of meaning.

This young Chinese writer operates with at least three conceptions of spelling, judging from his writing: with the newly learned alphabetic system, with his previously learned Chinese system of characters (which he is very likely **still** learning), and, when these two do not suffice, with a system of spelling ideas/concepts by use of images directly. Now it is impossible to know from this example which of these is dominant. What is clear is that he has a complex (set of) system(s) for spelling at his disposal; that he feels entirely free to be creative with the resources he has; and that, perhaps first and foremost, spelling for him is about **putting meaning on paper**.

It may be as well to adopt that as the general principle: spelling is about making meaning, in any of a number of different ways. This applies to reading as much as to writing. When on a train journey in Sweden recently I saw the word *Bandistrikt*. I attempted to 'read' this word: that is, to make sense of it. In order to do so I had to 'spell' it for myself: I had to decide what its internal structure is. My first analysis was based on my preconceptions about what Swedish words are like in their phonological and syllabic structure. I thought 'Yes, there's a part I recognize: *trikt*, which left me with *Bandis*. I couldn't make any sense of *Bandis*; what could *bandis* be? What could **a** bandis be? Only after some little while did I connect the word with the fact that is was written on the side of an engineering railway carriage. I then re-analysed it as *Ban* and *distrikt*. My reading could only proceed and was based on a spelling – right or wrong – in which meaning, both the 'meaning' of the syllabic structure of Swedish (as it exists in my imagination) and the meaning of the words of Swedish (*Ban* = (rail)way, *distrikt* = district), provided the essential basis.

To answer the question posed at the beginning of this section, spelling is a recording of meaning, where meaning can have many different forms: the meaning of the sound, the meaning of an intonation, the meaning of a syllabic system, or the meaning of a word. Sometimes this recording is the externalization of a meaning from our brain – from our memories – constantly remade, as when I write/spell a word that I know well. Sometimes the recording is a re-recording, a transposition from one system to another: from sound to graphic matter, for instance. Spelling always involves meaning. What meanings are 'allowed into' spelling, and what meanings are recognized, and what re-recordings and transpositions count and which do not, are matters settled more or less firmly by conventions of the moment.

Children play with these conventions. In the kind of 'joke' of which Figure 0.2 is an example, sound-as-meaning is the issue.

Of course children also 'play' with these conventions much more seriously, and constantly work with and against them. Much of this book is precisely about that. And just like the young writer from Hong Kong, they are entirely happy to develop visual symbols as a means for spelling the meanings that they want to express.

Knock, knock.	Knock, knock.
Who's there?	*Who's there?*
Scot.	Ammonia.
Scot who?	*Ammonia who?*
Scot nothing to do with you.	Ammonia little boy who can't reach the doorbell.

These are parallelled, at the level of meaning, by equally countless 'what do you get if . . .' jokes as in these examples.

What do you get if you cross a tiara with a motorway?
A jewel carriageway.

What do you get if you cross a citrus fruit with a doctor?
Lemon-aid.

These visual symbols or visual icons seem different in kind from the 'images' that, of course, they also draw constantly. They seem, rather, more like the development of elements in a quite formal lexicon – 'visual words' in a way. I have in my 'collection' no end of these: drawings of an object, frequently a human figure, drawn over and over again, usually with small variations always in the same size, often framed by a drawn frame or by the shape of a usually small piece of paper (Figure 0.3).

0.2 Routes into spelling

Children have many routes into spelling, and all children always use more than just one. Meaning, however, is an absolutely essential element in all of these routes, and unless we realize this we cannot understand children's spellings. And here one huge problem is our adult conception of **meaning**: whether the formal concept as developed in philosophy or in linguistics, or far less formal, everyday concepts of meaning. Children see meaning in everything; they endow everything with meaning, in a truly magical way; and they make meaning with all available means, of which the means of spelling, letters mainly, are just one. For children sound is or has meaning (as in the 'colour', or quality, of sound); sounds have meaning, as in the sound qualities of any part of the natural or social environment; and shape has meaning, as in the jagged edge or the smooth curve; etc. Meaning is a central component of all their routes.

Figure 0.2 Visual icons: littel monster

Spelling, probably for all children, starts as the making of visible traces: a line drawn to accompany the telling of an unfolding event, or the developing of a description. Spelling, we might say, starts as – or with – writing: this is **writing** both as the making of marks that 'stand for' things in the world ('This is a bear, the bear is growling' said while drawing a complex line/pattern), and as the imitation of writing that we all know so well from children anywhere in the world where alphabetic writing systems are in common, public use. Nearly always this 'writing' starts on the child's own initiative, entirely unremarkably, in just the same way as she or he will draw, build, glue, paint, cut or sing: simply as a way of being in the world, interacting with a particular bit of the world, making meaning in and around and with a bit of the world. Frequently therefore the child's name, or that of a parent or friend, will figure largely in this early writing.

But the important point is that spelling starts as writing: as an activity starting with – concerned with – the graphic/visual, a making of a particular kind of 'picture'. And at this point the emphasis is on the **look** of writing, and on getting that look right, whatever the feature may be that the child has happened to focus on. This initial identity of writing and spelling is important to bear in mind: children are focused on **writing**, and remain focused on writing, long before they ever become interested in **spelling**. **Spelling** is the school's interest, as is writing of course, but **writing** is much more the child's interest. Long before they go to school, children will ask 'How do you write Kashmir?' (or any significant name or word), never 'how do you spell . . .'. This emphasis on writing remains, and the emphasis on writing is of course an emphasis on meaning.

When spelling emerges on the horizon of the child's attention, usually as a schooled activity, it tends to appear as a highly formal activity. **Meaning** recedes from the centre of attention, and concern with formal rules, which are not focused on meaning, takes over. Spelling appears as a code for establishing relations between sound substance and graphic substance – between speech sounds and letters. This code, as we all know, is a complex one, and later in the book I suggest that it is the history of the English language as well as the history of the alphabet itself that is the reason for this. For children the consequence is that their preferred route – a route via meanings – is officially closed off, and a new route, that of the code of spelling, opens up.

Predictably, children respond differentially to spelling-as-a-code. Most children love codes and playing with codes; but they expect codes to work, to be logical, to be predictable, to have regularity, dependability. They expect to be able to crack the code; and they are expert code-crackers. The codes that they invent constantly – to govern play, to encode meanings – are dependable. The code of spelling is not a fully dependable code; and it is anything but logical. Many children therefore turn away from an initial interest in spelling-as-a-code; and the more there is an insistence on learning the code, and the more there is an insistence on this code as really logical and dependable, the more the **real** code-crackers will refuse to be interested.

Other children have a greater tolerance of messiness, of unpredictability, of things just having to be accepted as they are. They are more likely to stay with an interest in spelling than those whose interest actually is in codes. Overlaying this fundamental difference in their approach to the phenomenon of spelling is then a whole host of other possible routes – via the look of spelling, via sound, via words as whole entities, via syllable patterns, via rhyme, etc.

This picture is made infinitely more complex by the fact that the spelling-as-a-code approach is founded on an approach that requires an implausible view of language: a view of language as stable, as homogeneous, of **one** language spoken by all those who need to make the relation between sound and letter. The facts of dialect, and the fact of language as infinitely varying – within a very broad range of relative stability – complicates spelling enormously. Any 'rules' of spelling will only ever apply to one dialect of English. If a school teaches one such set of rules, and if its population consists of speakers who come from a diversity of linguistic backgrounds – even if just those of varieties of English – then some children will have infinitely greater problems than others.

Children want to please – give or take the occasional tantrum. In relation to spelling children strive enormously hard to 'get it right'. Children are also blessed – barring pathologies of some kinds – with the most acute hearing. Insofar as spelling is the recording of the sound of speech by means of letters, children provide the most ingenious solutions to recording **accurately**, **precisely**, what they have actually heard. In this book I provide lots of examples of this. It has occurred to me that it would be possible to use children's spellings as highly accurate data to document the actual precise sounds of – let's say in this case an English dialect – in a particular locality. Their spellings could be taken as reliable data documenting the characteristics of spoken English in a specific locality, at a particular time.

From this, I have made for myself a distinction that seems important to me, between **accurate spelling** and **correct spelling**. Just about all children spell accurately: that is, they represent via letters what it is they have heard, or what it is they want to indicate as the sound to be made, or as the meaning they wish to convey in sounds. Of course, this accurate spelling does not usually coincide with the **correct** spelling, the spelling on which a community's conventions insist. This leaves the pedagogical problem of how to bring the two into harmony without merely imposing the correct form.

To me it seems that the idea of accurate spelling can become an essential pedagogical insight in the aim of getting children to **correct spelling**. For one thing, it forces us to take the child seriously, and to engage with her or him as serious, as striving to do the very best; and it provides an insight into the child's thinking, into her or his 'logic'. The focus on correct spelling alone reduces most of the intelligent work of children to mere error, incomprehensible and often rubbish. That cannot possibly be motivating for any child; worse, it overlooks the very intelligence and creativity that we need to foster.

0.3 Spelling in a changing world

The world is not standing still; indeed, we are blessed or cursed to be living in a period of intense change – perhaps more intense change than any in the last 700 or 800 years. Multiculturalism is changing the linguistic composition of societies; and technology is changing the means of communication, as much as the modes of economic production. Technology, multiculturalism, the new economies of information and services, in the context of globalization (itself an effect of technologies of information transport), are making image more significant than writing in many domains of public communication. In this context the relation of spoken and written language is coming under new, intense strains, and these will have their effects on spelling. For one thing, the new technologies of direct voice interaction with computing devices will make available new routes to making speech visible, not handled by the hand and the pen, or by the hand and the keyboard. This will have the most profound effects on what we think writing is, and on what writing will become. Writing will newly come under the control of speech; writing will, in the very near future, be speech displayed on a screen. The whole vast machinery of spelling regulation will very likely be unmade or remade by this move.

At the same time this same screen – no longer the page, the hitherto dominant site of writing – is the domain of the image, of the visible as image. One consequence of this, already noticeable everywhere, is that writing will become much more affected by visual considerations. And a new visuality, a new iconicity, will come into writing: the innovation of the child from Hong Kong, the visual lexicon of the five-year old girl, will become commonplace.

And that future is not somewhere in the distance. It is the future of the next decade; certainly it is the future of the lifetimes of those now in school. In that context it becomes essential to think in truly profound ways about spelling, and about how our schools should approach spelling. Are unreflecting impositions of ideas of spelling as governed by fixed codes likely to serve the young in their lives? Are such notions likely to make them into the innovators that they will need to be?

Chapter 1

Why, and why now?

1.1 The contemporary debate

It is a Saturday in January, and I am strolling through the market in an outer suburb of North London. At a flower stall I see a sign on a pot-plant: *Cyclemen £1.50.*
I have been thinking about spelling for some months now, and so I make a men-
tal note of this small example. On the same day, in the same market, I can see
any number of examples of what in London is called the 'barrow boy's apostrophe'. *Tom's £1 a pound, Cue's 3 for £1.50, Chrys's 3 bunches £2.50.* The latter is well
recognized, and it is the subject of some mild humour. It is also the object of eval-
uation: the barrow boy's apostrophe is clearly a sign of being working class, and
of being – let's put it bluntly – 'uneducated'. The educated person's confident
judgement settles the matter; no particular harm is or seems to be done; the structure of the social world is reaffirmed; and that is that.

Of course, as someone interested in the issue, I can't quite leave it there. For
one thing, there are many occasions when the decision to confirm the shape of
the social world does leave someone at a disadvantage. The barrow boy's apostrophe is one thing when it appears on the barrow or on the shelves of the greengrocer (quite ubiquitously in Britain, as in Australia); it is another thing entirely
in the letter of a job application. The judgement, 'uneducated', remains the same;
its consequences change.

There is, as always, another way to look at *cyclemen*, at *Tom's, Cue's, Chrys's* and
Cauli's. That is to ask 'What are these writers trying to convey with their spelling?'
I suspect that the vendor selling the cyclamen (is the plural cyclamen or cycla-
mens?) wasn't actually confused about what it was that he was offering for sale.
But he knew the word *cycle* as in *bicycle*, and he didn't know a word such as *cycla*,
and so he normalized the spelling, probably quite inadvertently. I suspect that
whenever he had heard the word *cyclamen* before, he had imagined – in fact I want
to say 'visualized' – its written form just as he had spelled it here.

This is the strategy that all of us use, constantly; though if we are 'well educated', and particularly if we are of a certain age and we think that our writing
matters, we might verify our assessment by looking in a dictionary before we com-
mit ourselves to a spelling in public. Certainly it is the strategy that all children

must use, because for them every word is new at some stage in their move into literacy. But then, while this strategy may not be all that educated, it actually is highly rational. It is pragmatic, even if as a strategy it responds to an entirely different set of criteria from mine, which are focused on different value systems: not so much on **communication** as here in the market, as on a certain self-definition – precisely as careful and as well educated.

If we applied this same way of looking to the barrow boy's apostrophe, we might also change our assessment. *Tom's* might be the misapplied apostrophe of the (vestiges of the) possessive case in English; though it might more plausibly be a sign of an abbreviation of *Tom[atoe]s*, where the apostrophe marks the missing letters, as it does in *Amy's 'Ardware* (on a shop in East London) or, more conventionally, in the 'it's' of 'It's hardly worth arguing', or of the 'wasn't' as in 'It wasn't worth what we paid for it'. The use of some graphic mark to indicate a contraction (or an elision) has a very long history in English, as in other languages (the **accent circumflex** as in '*îlot*' (islet) marking a formerly present 's' for instance).

We might still wish to persuade the greengrocer, the barrow boy, or the Académie française to change their practice. We couldn't maintain, however, that these were uses without their own rhyme or reason. We might still apply the judgement 'uneducated', but it could no longer mean acting without well-thought-out principle. The fact that we are very quick with adverse judgement is not unrelated to the fact that these writers occupy a certain social and cultural place.

In Australia greengrocers have, over the last two or three decades, tended to be Australians of Southern European, Middle Eastern, and more recently, South East Asian origin. In England (I do mean England, not Britain) they have tended to be (lower) working class, and often from particular localities: the Cockney, for instance. Judgements are easily made by the 'well educated' middle class on people from such backgrounds (I first heard the term 'barrow boy's apostrophe' used by a very middle-class academic in a higher education institution devoted to teacher education). Neither *cyclemen* nor *Tom's* points to being well educated; but it certainly doesn't point to being incompetent in communication either.

Concerns over spelling wax and wane, from which fact we might deduce that it is all just a matter of fashion. For instance, neither of my older children, now in their late twenties, is what we might call a 'good' or 'competent' or 'confident' speller. The reason, as we are all aware, is that their generation went through school in a period when concern with spelling was actually seen as negative, as a stifling of creativity and expressiveness, and perhaps even as authoritarian: not what the school (they both had their early schooling in England and then in Australia) saw itself as being about. Their teachers attended to their spelling, but never heavily. Our second lot of children are experiencing the new climate of the 1990s, in which achievement in such matters is very highly valued, and in which achievement in things such as spelling (together with 'numeracy') is threatening to become all that education is about.

One of the points of this book is to show that concern with spelling is not about fashion, but about anxieties produced by wider and deeper social, cultural and economic changes, which are finding one form of expression in this particular issue. The 1960s (and the early 1970s) was a period of confidence in the so-called 'West': a period of economic success, of political confidence, of military superiority. In such a period, conformity, adherence to convention and anxieties about difference are not in the foreground, and do not need to form a part of the educational agenda. If that suggestion supplies at least one part of an explanation for the lack of concern at that time, it can also form at least one part of an explanation for the concerns we are experiencing now. The freedom of the 1960s and, at least, the early part of the 1970s has gone. A whole range of factors – foremost amongst these economic and cultural – have changed. The governments of nation states have seen control over the economy slip away from them as an effect of the globalization of finance capital. This change, along with others – the disappearance of heavy industries, and with them of forms of employment on which Western economies had been built – has brought radical insecurity, uncertainty and anxiety. This is a time to seek stability, certainty and security; and, as so often, language use and all other aspects of linguistic practice come to serve as powerful metaphors for the reimposition of stability and control.

Concern with spelling, we can safely say, is never a matter of fashion. In a very different way, and at a much earlier time in English history, spelling became a social and political tool in the development of a 'national' language. Anyone reading texts in Early Modern English, say the Paston letters (from the mid to late fifteenth century), will find spellings that are anything but 'uniform'. They reflect characteristics of the regional dialects (East Anglian in this case), and they show what seems to us now an astonishing and seemingly idiosyncratic variation between writers. That variation was in no way an impediment to communication. However, in the later sixteenth and early seventeenth centuries it became the focus of the attention of successive generations of grammarians: the so-called inkhorn grammarians, whose energies went into the production of word books in which spelling became 'regularized', made to be 'consistent'. The fact that their efforts coincided with the centralization and modernization of the British state under the Tudors was no coincidence.

Of course, the accompanying factor of the translation of the King James Version of the Bible provided one hugely significant common text – as had Luther's Bible in Germany previously. Nor can the technological factor of the somewhat earlier introduction of printing with movable type be overstressed here: a reminder that technology then, as now, has had and will have profound effects. Then, it provided one essential means for the success of the drive to uniformity; now, its effects are likely to be more profound, though not yet settled.

Spelling, it bears repeating, is not a matter of fashion. The real task facing us is that of understanding the grounds of our contemporary concerns. On that depends the development of effective answers and solutions to the problems of which current anxieties over literacy are one symptom. This cannot happen unless the problem is understood and tackled at a more profound level than that at which it appears in public debates. That is what this book attempts to do.

1.2 Education, literacy and the economy

Let me focus on just one of the central issues affecting and shaping this debate at the moment: the economy. There are others, such as the globalization and internationalization of the media, and of culture more generally; but here I shall set those aside. It is clear that Western, technologically developed societies are in the middle of the most far-reaching economic changes. Formerly foundational industries have either disappeared (coal mining, shipbuilding, steelmaking) or changed in profound fashion (the automation of car manufacturing, of textiles, of banking). The dispositions, skills and knowledges that were essential to those industries have disappeared, including whatever literacy and language skills the jobs in those industries entailed – usually, and for the mass of the workers, quite rudimentary skills as far as literacy was concerned. These industries were stable, with stable job hierarchies and relatively stable work practices. Consequently, the skills and knowledges were stable; indeed, a disposition of stability (as one kind of dependability) was a desired and basic requirement in the workforce.

These forms of industry have disappeared; or, to be more precise, they no longer form either the foundational sector of the economy or the basis of ways of thinking about economic life. Yet forms of education, of organization of schools – whether that of the school day or year, or of curricula, including literacy – were developed precisely to mesh with and provide the necessary forms of labour for those industries, with the required skills and dispositions. To a very large extent schools are still organized in relation to this form of the economy – which no longer exists. This applies to curricula of literacy, spelling included, as much as to other aspects of schooling.

The newer forms of the economy, based on information and on services, already exist, and they will continue to expand in ways that are not entirely knowable. It will be an economy based on information in the widest possible sense; and this information will be represented and communicated through a wide range of modes: with images of all kinds; with language as speech and as writing; and with numbers. It will also – necessarily – be an economy in which culture plays a central role, in all forms, whether in the explosion of the domains of leisure, in PR, in marketing or in 'services' of all kinds. This new economy demands its specialized modes of communication, and, as well as those just mentioned, demands uses of sound (whether as music or as soundtrack), uses of 3D representations, greater uses of images, and so on. Paradoxically, despite our intense current concerns with 'literacy', writing in many of its traditional forms will become less significant in many sectors of that new economy. 'Visualization' represents one of the major drives for electronic industries, and the visual will reconfigure our societies' uses of language – whether as speech or as writing – quite fundamentally.

This new information-based economy relates in the most direct and subtle ways to the new information and communication technologies, and these are anything but stable at present. Whereas the former economic situation was marked by the stability of practices, of structures and of identities, this new situation is the antithesis of all these, and is likely to be so for a considerable time to come. So, rather than the need to acquire stable skills and knowledges in the form of conventional speech and writing-based skills, what is now required is to develop skills and knowledges of an entirely flexible kind. The identities and personal dispositions that will be most highly valued, and most essential, will be those of flexibility, creativity and innovation. This is the defining context in which to think about spelling and the teaching of spelling.

The education systems of anglophone societies of the present period are not equipped to deal with these new requirements, and, in nearly all of their structures, are not in alignment with these needs. Nor do the ever more insistent urgings of politicians point in this direction, superficial appearances not withstanding. Many of the current attmepts at experimentation with schooling (I am writing this in the first half of 1998) are attempts to deal with entirely new demands by tinkering with old structures. It is as though the Wright brothers, having glimpsed the possibility of powered flight, were now setting about designing a state-of-the-art steam engine as the motive power for this future form of transport. The education system now educates the vast majority of young people right through to the age of seventeen or eighteen, when many of them will join higher education. What had been a system designed to produce a mass-labour force for the former economy on the one hand and an élite for its professional requirements on the other, is now attempting to deal with the mass of the population with the same means, assumptions, processes, practices and structures as it had for the élite. It is not surprising that this system is creaking to the point of breaking. In this context, talk of declining standards is simply beside the point.

In the meantime the external environment for which the education system had prepared the young has vanished, and is being replaced in largely unknowable and uncontrollable ways by a new environment. The former economy, which produced jobs for nearly all, no longer exists. These were jobs for a largely male workforce; very many of the new jobs are for (or are taken up by) women. In any case, the workforce that is still being produced by institutional education is not necessarily the workforce needed in this new environment. Yet the new economy has to make do, largely, with a workforce produced to meet former requirements, and to cope with a serious mismatch between older dispositions and skills and new requirements.

Education systems around the anglophone world are being blamed by their governments for a state of affairs that is of neither's making. Globalization of finance has taken economic control from national governments. Governments, responding to the electorate's expectation that they should govern, turn the blame on institutional education, on the teaching profession, on parents and on children. In a bizarre turn, the best solution that seems available to politicians and many public commentators is to march resolutely back to an assumed known and golden past held up as a new future – or to cobble unsteady planks to the future out of the edifice of the present structure.

The frames that held education together as a stable system of practices with stable values and knowledges, invisibly but seemingly unshakeable. Examples are the frame of the nation state and of its values; of forms of the economy; of social arrangements, such as gender (and family) structures; of certainties about knowledge and its value. All these are coming undone. Further, the centrality of language as writing, so long the foundational medium of schooling and of 'Western' education, is coming under increasing challenge, whether in its assumed relation to thinking and learning, to kinds of knowledge, and to forms of rationality, or as the major mode of public communication. In part this is a corollary of the fact that in many domains of public and economic life, and not just of the print and electronic media, images are now used as the central means of information and communication.

Clearly this will have effects on conceptions of what literacy is. At the moment the older, more conventional versions of literacy – alphabetic writing – are still seen as the central issue in education. This is hardly surprising. Society's most significant knowledge is held in verbal literacy; the social groups who control that knowledge also control the forms of literacy; and they define themselves, their identity – who they are – through this form of literacy. Given that their own notions of self, their value systems, are so closely dependent on it, it is hardly surprising that it should continue to be valued in this way. Nevertheless, it is this older, conventional form that is now changing in its uses and in its characteristics.

What, then, is the relation between literacy and the economy, and therefore between spelling – as one aspect of literacy – and the economy? Some links are obvious and have been asserted continuously: for instance, the obvious needs of written communication in all sectors of the economy. But that seems so superficial – even if unquestionably important – that one would hardly want to waste breath talking about it: it is too obviously significant and it is actually relatively easy to attend to and to fix. It is not worth spending more words on the topic.

For me the important connection lies at a much deeper level. If the older economy and its structures and practices displayed stabilities of the kind I mentioned earlier, then it needed these stabilities in terms of skills and knowledges on the one hand, **and**, in terms of forms of identity, of what people were like, on the other. To put it crudely, if what was needed in the world of jobs was people who at one level were reliably, dependably able to carry out undemanding, repetitive jobs day in, day out, and who, given the outline of a simple task, would be prepared to carry it out without fail, or who at another level would adhere to the stable practices of trades or of professions, then that was what the education system had to produce. If the new information-based economies need skills, knowledges and dispositions of flexibility, adaptability, creativity and innovation, then the question is: how can the education system meet these new demands? Is the teaching of spelling by rote, as a fixed system with illogical but rigid rules, which must be adhered to without challenge or understanding, a plausible route to engender such dispositions? Clearly no. Yet we do want children to be confident spellers. How do we proceed?

1.3 Spelling

In the chapters that follow I shall explore in detail what this thing 'spelling' is. My answer – not difficult to predict – is that it is a good deal more complex, and more interesting, than it appears in the pronouncements of many experts and non-experts, in the media or elsewhere. But here I want to make a different and prior point. Spelling is a complex set of practices, and how it is handled in education not only tells us much about the real purposes and aims of the education system and of those whose wishes control it, but also has fundamental effects on how the young who experience the teaching and learning of it will come to see themselves, and will think about themselves and their world. Spelling is one of those practices, in themselves insignificant, that have the most profound consequences.

I have suggested that past forms of the economy – perhaps well-enough characterized by the two 'isms' of Fordism and Taylorism – needed dispositions from the major proportion of the workforce of dependability, stability, of a willingness to do the same simple act over and over. Henry Ford founded his success on fitting humans to the mechanical repetitions of the production line. F. W. Taylor perfected twentieth-century managerialism by examining and – timing – the minute steps of (bureaucratic) production processes. He extended this from the production line to the office, and so a common ethos, a uniform ideology, took hold, in which the assumption that all complex processes could be broken down into simple, knowable, measurable and *repeatable* steps, and that humans could be trained to adapt themselves as parts to such rigid processes, became an unshakeable and 'natural' commonsense.

Of course, ideas of such extent and magnitude never occur in isolation; they are always the expression of larger ideas, which 'are about' in a general sort of way. It is neither an accident nor a surprise that much of twentieth-century thinking about language was quite compatible – similar, really, at an abstract level – with such ideas about social organization and economic work. Mainstream twentieth-century thinking about language focused on identifying clearly definable elements in the complex system of language. These clearly defined elements were seen as fitting together to make the larger, more complex structures. Twentieth-century linguistics was by and large (there are some important exceptions, though their ideas did not become dominant, on the whole, in 'mainstream' thinking) concerned with identifying small units that 'made up' larger units: identifying the units of sound, and then identifying the units which make up a sentence. The former was, broadly, the study of phonemics or phonology – the study of the regularities of sound in language – underpinned by the study of phonetics – the study of the material (physical) characteristics of speech sounds, and of their modes of production and reception. The latter was the study of grammar, and it comprised the study of **morphology** – the identification of the smallest meaningful units of language – and of **syntax** – the identification of the 'constituent' elements of clauses and sentences, and the description of the rules of their combination. Complexity – whether in industrial production, in large bureaucracies or in a (social) phenomenon such as language – was seen as a matter of identifying clearly definable simple elements, and of fitting these together in the appropriate manner, in larger, more complex structures.

This effort coincided with a somewhat paradoxial view and practice in relation to speech and writing. The common belief held by theoretical linguists tended to be that speech was 'language' in its primary form, and that writing was a secondary, derived form, invented or developed as a means of recording speech, for whatever purposes. This meant that the real effort of linguistics should be directed towards the understanding and description of speech. In this view the act of writing was an act of transcription: simply, speech transcribed into visible form. The science of phonology had established what the significant, stable sounds (the phonemes) of a particular language were: for instance the sound *k* as in *king*. In collaboration with phonetics, it had also described what variants of these phonemes occurred in different sound environments, and in different dialects. For instance *k* as in *king* has an audible escape of air following it (it is **aspirated**, in technical terms); but the *k* sound in *bickering*, or at the end of a word as in *lick it off* does not, in most people's speech, have that escape of air – the two *k* sounds are, in reality, quite distinct sounds. Or, to demonstrate a dialect difference: the short *oo* sound as in southern English pronunciations of *butcher* is pronounced as an *a* (as in *butler*) in certain northern English dialects. Work in phonology has provided a precise picture of the sounds and sound-variants in specific languages, and in their dialects.

The enterprise of describing the phonemes of a language supported, broadly speaking, the assumption that letters were the visible graphic equivalents of the core sounds – the phonemes – of a language. In English, as we all know, this assumption doesn't work at all well; in certain other European languages it works much more adequately – in Italian or Spanish, for instance.

The view that speech is language in its primary form, and the practices associated with that view, was not in itself paradoxical; indeed it looked (despite certain awkwardnesses) relatively unproblematic and straightforward. The paradox emerged with a split in Western linguistics between those who studied sounds and those who studied syntax and grammar. In Western linguistics, phonologists obviously studied the sounds of language-as-speech; syntacticians, however, studied the rules of syntax, and the morphology of its elements – 'grammar', broadly speaking – but did so by looking at **written** language. This seemed defensible as a practice as long as writing was regarded as the transliteration of speech. Over this century, the study of syntax emerged as the major theoretical area of linguistic inquiry. However, it is quite clear that in 'literate' societies writing develops quite distinct forms of syntax over time, and with its uses in specific environments. With this the paradox emerged: on the one hand the assertion that speech is language in its primary, in its essential form; and on the other hand the high-status practice of syntactic theory, in which the focus is on the written form of the language.

From the point of view of literacy this largely unacknowledge paradox has had far-reaching and severe consequences for generations of thinking about this issue, and for generations of teachers dealing with it. Most of all, it has had severe and often debilitating consequences for generations of children coming into the learning of writing with their own experience and meeting, in school, a common-sense quite at odds (my inclination is to say 'totally at odds') with their own felt and lived experience. In later chapters I make some further comments and qualifications on this; here I shall leave my point in this stark form, except to point to one fact. Speech exists in the medium of sound, and is governed by time: that is, sounds happen one at a time. Writing exists in the medium of graphic form (dependent on the medium of light), and is governed by space: that is, letters are displayed on the space of the page or wherever. The move from sound to graphic form is therefore also a move from the logic of temporal sequence to the logic of spatial display. Some of the severest problems encountered in the learning of writing – dyslexia, for instance – may well be due to this profound shift.

To put the consequences for thinking about literacy in a nutshell: speech and writing are profoundly different in much of their grammatical and syntactic organisation. In the context of this paradoxical environment, it has been this unrecognized confusion about language – Is language to be equated with the structures and forms of speech? Or is it to be equated with the forms and structures of writing? – that has led to lack of clarity, to inaccuracy, to deep and unrecognized confusion, both for linguistics and for education.

From the point of view of spelling, the (unacknowledged) priority of language in the written form has led to the paradox in which it is asserted that spelling is a system for transliterating sound into graphic form, a move from speech-sound to letter, from speech to writing; yet where it is also assumed – entirely unself-consciously, implicitly, and without recognition of this issue – that writing is 'first', that the 'spelling' of a word is as it is in writing. Because of that, the graphic transcriptions of speech as they appear in the written form really have to be known to the 'speller' already before she or he speaks and then spells the word. The written language is the norm, the stable basis; speech and spoken forms are mapped onto it. One could nearly say that in a 'literate culture' speech is the spelling of writing. That is, in as far as spelling is the knowledge of correspondences between sounds and graphic form, between something that is audible and something that is visible, it is the existence and the knowledge of the visible written form that guarantees the correct spelling. For instance, if I want to 'check' a spelling, I need to know where to go in the dictionary: I need to have a visual image of the word, of what the visible shape (as sequences of letters) of a word is.

Now, in the way I've put it here, the assertion sounds bizarre; no one expects a child learning to write of to spell to know beforehand what the written form looks like. Spelling rules are meant to be rules that tell you how to get from the spoken to the written form. In fact, spelling rules work, always provided that you already know what the written form is like. That is the implicit assumption, as I hope to show.

This may be fine for someone who is 'in' the system. From the learner's point of view the problem is that she or he has no visible correlate for the sounded word, nor even necessarily a sense of what the word is – no image of the word as a picture of a sequence of letters. So a 'rule' such as '*e* at the end of *fame* makes the vowel longer' is useless as a rule for spelling, if spelling means turning sound into graphic marks; it has a use as a rule for 'sounding', for transliterating graphic marks into sound. The rule works one way, for turning written language into sound. But it is not a rule for turning sound into graphic marks. The rule assumes that I have a picture of the written word in my mind's eye, that I want to sound it, and that what I'm wondering about is what the function of the *e* at the end of the word might be. For learners of spelling the unacknowledged priority of the written form, and the expression of rules in those terms, is a fundamental problem.

To see what I have in mind, consider Example 1.1 on pp 20–21, the spelling, by a 6-year-old, of the word *sharpeners*. She knows what the word sounds like, but she doesn't have a 'picture' of the graphic representation available to her.

As I say, the rough sketch of assumptions that I have drawn may seem bizarre; but I believe it corresponds closely to what is the case. If my sketch has validity, then the question that it raises most immediately is 'How could this situation have lasted so long, if it is so deeply misconceived?'. My answer, to restate it, is largely that a particular view of language has held nearly unchallenged sway for a very long time. That view has seen language as stable; as primarily writing; as consisting of knowable and describable small elements, which are put together to make larger elements – a building-block view of language. It has therefore insisted on the reality of a correspondence between clearly definable spoken elements and clearly knowable graphic elements (even if in some languages, such as English, the correspondence had become a bit 'murky').

Moreover, this view accorded with other larger-level and widespread views about the way society itself and its economy was (and could be) understood and organized. More still, if Fordism was in fact the way that it undoubtedly was, and if Taylorism provided a good means of managing Fordism – whether in car manufacturing, in the typing pool or in large bureaucracies – and if these arrangements produced work, wealth, development, stability (ignoring massive hiccups such as the Great Depression), then it would be entirely normal that the education system should mirror these arrangements. Indeed, it was necessary that it should do so.

Of course, social theorists (and others) knew that things were always a bit more complex than the theory or the ideology suggested, and managers would fear that things could slither away from under their control. And, of course, phoneticians and phonologists knew that speech was variable, whether as social or as regional dialect, and that sounds were variable in their different environments. Most of them knew that the phoneme was a useful abstraction and, as such, a fiction.

Textbooks in linguistics of the period are full of examples that show this, and, at the same time, they are also full of ways in which the prevailing commonsense about language could be salvaged. The theories, and the social and economic givens,

Example 1.1

Is spelling a matter of sight or of sound?

Is spelling a matter of sight or of sound? A matter of **seeing** the **letter shape** of a word, or a matter of accurately **hearing** the **sound shape** of a word?

Whichever decision we make, the rules of spelling need to be stated in terms of the starting point we have chosen. In this example I focus on the matter of the (absent) *r* in the letter shape of the word, or of the vowel sound in the spoken form.

If we choose **sight** (the **look** of a word) as the starting point, the rule might say: a sequence such as *ar* in *sharpener* can be said with a long *a* sound, especially when it is followed by a consonant such as *p* (or *k* or *t*).

But beware:

> Letter shapes such as *bath, far, dance, hard* and others also produce the long *a* sound.

> In many dialects letter shapes such as *far, hard* produce the same long *a* sound but are followed by a more or less strongly articulated *r*. In other words, the rule applies to one dialect, Standard English; it does not apply in the same way to all dialects of English.

> In some pronunciations, the *ar* in *sharpener* becomes just *a*, but the *ar* in *sharp* might have the *r* pronounced.

If we choose **hearing**, **accurate** hearing (the **sound** of the word), as the starting point, then really the first question is: What did the child actually hear? What dialect was spoken? In this instance she is likely to have had as her model her parents' Australian English; and she will have heard a sound shape without the *r*. The second step would be to ask: Does the spelling rule make sense in terms of the dialect that the child (or the children in a class) hears (or hear)?

In Standard English a sound shape such as *sha:p* tends to be transliterated into *sharp*; but *sha:ft* does not become *sharft*, *la:f* (laugh) does not become *larf*, and so on for the sounds in *bath, France, answer, are, castle, cast, . . .*

In other words, the rule for the teacher should be: first know your dialect and the children's dialect; then understand the difference between the sound shape in the child(ren)'s dialect and that of the standard; and teach the spelling rule, being sensitive to that difference. Children will often need to learn some general rule; they will also need to be prepared for learning by rote the letter shapes of many words.

Historically, the *r* in *sharp* comes from an old English form, *shearfan*, in which the *r* was pronounced, as it still is in its near relations, such as German *schärfen*.

| white shoes | vait ʃuːs |
| why choose | vai tʃuːs |

Setig by the fiuir
Pies Cold and sheviring
Vedig a book look a reaiwd
thes a Cipe of Tea

Sitting by the fire place
cold and shivering
reading a book (I) look around
there's a cup of tea

Example 1.2

In ordinary, informal speech, words are more often than not said without any 'gap' between them, as a continuous string of sounds. In the first half of this century, several generations of structuralist linguists tried to establish rules for deciding either how speakers of a language know where the 'gaps' are, **or**, given that there are some strings of sound that sound identical but consist of different words – *why choose* vs *white shoes*, for example – how speakers know which words are actually being spoken.

Of course, in one way the problem is non-existent: it is unlikely that, in context, a confusion could arise. But that still leaves the question of how speakers know how to make the segmentations of a continuous stream of sounds into discrete words, how the ear and the brain make that distinction.

The problem is not 'merely academic'. It is a very real problem for anyone who learns a foreign language, and it is not academic for children learning their own first language. Once you know the words, it's fine; you know the words. But before you know what the words are, you have a problem. It is the problem of which *I look around/look a reawd* is one instance; many other examples are given throughout this book.

existed in mutual support; there was nothing to be gained from unsettling that which was so solidly settled, and which provided such tangible rewards to so many.

Our contemporary situation, the social and the economic situation of now, and of the short- and medium-term future, is no longer like that in any way. The fact that neither our linguistic nor our educational commonsense has quite caught up with the realities of the newer situation is a problem, and particularly so in education. In linguistics there are now radical doubts about the older certainties, whether in phonology or in syntax and grammar. The real fluidity and dynamism of language now seem at best only partially, or by severe distortion, captured by the certainties of fixed, bounded, stable elements and structures. In the economic sphere, companies have long since flattened their (Taylorist) management structures, and have moved to dynamic management notions, such as the notion of the 'corporate culture'. But inclusion in and membership of a culture puts the individual into an entirely different positon from that of the alienated, rigidly limited unit of labour working at the production line. To be a member of a culture requires full knowledge, full participation, full responsibility for wide-ranging processes, and the ability to respond to the changes that are normal in the fluid entity that is a culture. Is is a very different set of demands from those made of the worker on the Fordist production line.

The older conceptions of language, and the assumptions and practices of spelling that formed a part of them, were not without their truth. It is possible to see and to describe language in that way; and, if you do, it is possible to teach language on these principles. This is especially so if the environment makes that seem completly plausible and commonsensical. But language can also be viewed as a fluid, dynamic phenomenon, which responds readily to the demands of its users. If we see it like that, then our focus shifts to change, to transformation. Then we can see that, in the constantly varying uses that they make of it, language is constantly being transformed by its users.

This more complex view of language conforms with the more complex view of the wider environment, a now accepted ecological view, in which companies develop their corporate cultures together with all the members of a culture, which individual members of that company must make their own. To teach language – and spelling – according to the older rules in this newer environment is to misunderstand what ought to be the present purposes of education. The former strategy educates for conformity: for fitting in and for carrying out, reliably, the simple or the complex actions repeated during all of the working day. Of course, many such jobs continue, for many people. But that form of work, and those kinds of tasks, no longer characterize and typify the present economic world; and it is most certainly not the shape of the world of tomorrow. In the newer information-based economy, the core of the economy, the practices and metaphors that give it definition, are deeply different. They are the metaphors of change, of creativity, innovation, difference. In our thinking about spelling, in its teaching and learning, we cannot afford to continue with metaphors that are deeply at odds with the facts as they are, and with the shape of the new environments.

1.4 Technology and cultural change

For the last 300 or so years, language in the form of writing has been the defin-itive medium of education, of knowledge, of rationality, of cultural achievement, of public communication and of power. To be excluded from writing has meant to be excluded from all these. During this period, the technology of movable type, whether in the print media or, more recently, via the typewriter, has been the dominant technology in communication. The present period, and by that I mean not much longer than the last ten, possibly fifteen years (small computers made their appearance in my workplace about then – just), is marked by an epochal change in technology. Movable type is being, has been, will certainly be replaced in industrially developed societies within another ten years. The implications of this are vast and impossible to assess, though one consequence is already plain: information is no longer stored in 'type' or in letters, but in electronic form, in 'bytes'. A word, a page, a chapter, a letter, a document, an address, can all be changed with no difficulty, no fuss, not much real work. The technology of the typewriter had demanded dispositions of absolute accuracy: if a typing error occurred at the bottom of a page then that whole page had to be redone (if the document was important), with all the economic and other costs attendant on that. This had called for routines in training (a cloth placed over the learner's hands, so that movement became automatic) that demanded precision and relia-bility at all times. The institution in which I work still conducts typing tests for 'secretarial' staff, in which speed and accuracy are still highly valued, even though the new technologies have nearly superseded not just the need for accuracy but also the whole set of practices that used to be described by the word *secretarial*.

Electronic storage holds more information and has more possibilities than I, as a layperson, can imagine or utilize. As well as other information, it holds infor-mation on the rules of spelling – my computer has a spell-checker, entirely unused in my case! – so that any document I have written on my computer (I still write books and longer papers by hand) can be checked for its spelling, and 'corrected' at an instant. The fact that I don't use 'my' spell-checker is not due to the fact that I am a 'reliable speller'; like most reasonably literate people I have a list of words about which I feel insecure – *personnel, commitment, occurrence, intended* and a few others. The reason I don't use it is that the spell-checker tells me to spell words in forms that I don't wish to use. It is telling me to conform to the rules of another culture, which is something I do not wish to do.

It is here where, in a quite trivial example, technology and cultural change come together. Partly because of electronic technologies we live in an age in which the boundaries around cultures are becoming increasingly permeable – whether through the electronically disseminated mass media, through the leisure and plea-sure industries, or through the Internet and e-mail. In this context the rules about 'proper behaviour', of which spelling is one instance, are now no longer controlled in one place, but are controlled in several places: in part still in my culture (I have to spell in ways that do not offend the audience in my immediate culture), in part by other considerations (I am told that 'program' is more economical or efficient than 'programme'), in part in many others (when I e-mail someone who lives in the US or in Australia, I know that what is proper 'here' may be improper, quaint, or plain silly 'there'). Spelling is one social convention among many. A social group may lay much or a little emphasis on this one convention. The point about the present, and certainly about the future, is that many social groups now make their often conflicting presence felt to me, in my place.

This is a trivial example, although with the advent of direct voice interaction with computers (which, as an 'appliance', may itself be anachronistic in another fifteen years in its present form) this form of control is likely to become more difficult for any one group. I can't be blamed if I speak to my computer and its spelling program has given offence to one of my readers! Of course, what this will mean is not that control has disappeared, but that it will move somewhere else, more than likely to either the voice (I will have to learn to speak in a machine-compatible way), or to features such as layout.

This brings me to the last point here. My interaction with the computer is, at the moment at least, conducted via a **screen**. It is a spatial–visual means of display, and as such **visuality** is perhaps more in the centre that it is with a **page**. This may be particularly so as features of layout can be changed with the same ease as can features of spelling, and perhaps even more drastically. The screen is fundamentally a unit for visual display and it is used for just that – visual display. In other words, visual aspects even of written text as such become more focal, and with that, of course, the possibility of new forms of aesthetics: questions such as 'What does your text **look** like?' just as much as 'What does your text **read** like?'.

The screen as a unit of visual display is also a place where images in a conventional sense make their appearance, both as the icons that are used to inform me about the instructions and the potentials of the machine, and as the content of my texts. The revolution in the wider landscape of communication, which is making images – the visual in general – much more significant as a means for communication, is both speeded up by the move from page to screen, and is a part of it. The question in the smaller frame of this book is: What will spelling become as an effect of these interrelated changes, of shifts in technology, culture, and our use in modes of representation – the shift, that is, from writing to image? And what consequences arise for the teaching of spelling to and the learning of spelling by, say, 5- to 7-year-olds, who will be living their adult lives in that changed environment?

Chapter 2

A Framework for thinking about the issues

2.1 What is this thing called language?

Before we can begin to get a sense of what 'spelling' is, we need to have some sense about this thing we call 'language'. As I shall show, it isn't at all clear what we mean by language, or what is included and what is excluded for different people and in various theories under that label. That makes it difficult to know what is to be included in 'spelling' and what is not. This seemingly simple word *spelling* proves to be quite a problem. So do we actually know what language is? Once we have a settled sense about that, we may be able to get nearer to a sense of what kinds of things are included in this activity called spelling, a sense of what it is that gets or could be spelled.

When I say 'what we mean by language' I do not intend to sketch a miniature theory of language here; rather, I want to point to some things that all of us know but may not think about in relation to spelling, and to point to some other things that tend not to be included in definitions of what language is: for instance, language as a visual pheonomenon, or the *look* of language.

I always like to get at these questions by looking at the history of a word. I think that if I have a sense of what a word has meant in the past – a sense of 'where it has been' in its history, a sense of origins, of what meanings it has brought from its past into its present – then I can get a better grasp of what meanings it may have now. A brief etymological enquiry reveals (as per *Skeat's Etymological Dictionary*) that *spelling* comes from a family of meanings (in languages such as Gothic, Old High German, and Anglo-Saxon) around 'a saying', 'a narrative', 'a fable', 'a myth'; or, more prosaically, in Old Saxon, 'a word'. It is related to meanings such as 'an incantation', 'a form of magic': as when witches 'cast a spell'. In its forms as a verb it is linked to 'narrate', 'tell', 'speak', 'declare'. One of its current relatives in Modern English is the word *gospel* – 'God's spel', the **word** of God.

This is an expansive history of meaning, and it faces in two directions: in the direction of the kinds of **things that are to be spelled** – a myth, a fable, an important word, or **the** word, an incantation; and in the direction of **how what is spelled is to be made known**, communicated, declared – the meanings of 'narrate', 'speak', 'tell', 'declare'. A spelling speaks and declares the meaning of that which is to be spelled.

That is not the now usual meaning of '*spelling*'; but as I hope to show, that is precisely the meaning of spelling that young humans use in trying to understand the means by which we can tell, declare, narrate, any number of hugely diverse things, in visible form, on paper or on some other convenient surface. For adults, spelling has become highly reduced in its meanings, by and large (though never exclusively) to something like: capturing the essentials of the characteristics of the sound of words in graphic form, via the means of letters.

Language, however, is much more than sound as in speech, or of graphic substance as in writing. In many ways we could say that sound is itself a spelling – a spelling of meanings, of ideas, of attitudes, feelings, dispositions. That would considerably extend our sense of what spelling is. It would bring in precisely the points made by my small etymological enquiry, that spelling is about **declaring**, about making visible and tangible, a vast range of meanings that are judged as significant. Above all it would show that this thing that we call language is first and foremost about meanings. That establishes a clear contrast with the now popular conception of spelling as sound transcribed into visible form, behind which stands one view of language, that language is sound, and that meaning in a productive sense doesn't enter into what we consider as spelling in any way at all.

In the early spellings of children their views of the matter can be seen very clearly. The multiplicity of the potential meanings of spelling are revealed when one looks at their efforts. Letters, especially the initial letters of the names of the young spellers, are often turned into pictures. So in Example 2.1, pp 32–1, the B of *Barney* becomes a picture of Barney; it becomes (the likeness of) Barney. This is straightforwardly an attempt to make letters conform to the child's principle that spelling is to declare (a) meaning, and that letters represent meanings. Here the meaning is, somehow, the meaning of 'me', 'my identity', 'my **self**'.

A quite different meaning is at issue in the alphabet charts often constructed by – though more usually for – young children: the 'Snake is for S' example, with the letter drawn as a snake (the letter as picture of an object), **and** a hissing sound coming from the snake (the letter as mimicking the sound for which it stands).

But even though one strong adult commonsense view is that language is sound and that spelling is the process of capturing that sound via the means of the alphabet, much, perhaps most, of the sound-substance of speech is never represented in spelling. The pitch fluctuations of the voice – the melody of the voice – which convey grammatical meanings (the falling voice-contour as statement; the rising voice-contour as question) as well as attitudinal/emotional meanings – with greater pitch movement serving as a sign of 'excitement', of intensity of attitude and of feeling, and small pitch movement as a sign of calmness, detachment, boredom – these are never transcribed; they are never 'spelled'. They may be 'written out', as in the novelist's 'she said excitedly, . . . calmly . . . lightly'. Nor do we spell the intensity of the sound, its loudness; nor the speed of our speech; nor its rhythmic features. These are all meaningful ('Don't raise your voice at me!'

'Slow down, you're too excited!'), but most of these (intonation used to mark a hesitant question or uncertain statement being borderline cases) are not included in our commonsense conception of what language is. Consequently, our cultures have not developed transcriptional means for them; they do not get spelled. However, such things are 'spelled' in musical scores, as we know: the gradual increase in loudness, the staccato or the pizzicato production of individual sounds, the increases or decreases in tempo, etc., all appear in musical scores. This shows quite clearly that these features can be spelled; the reason they are not is that in our commonsense conception of language they are not regarded as significant, whereas in music they are. Things that get too close to 'emotion' are, we might say, written out of language.

In other words, what gets 'spelled' is a quite narrow selection from the large range of sound features; and that selection is itself based on conceptions of what language is, and what is 'outside' language. It is difficult to be certain about this, but at times it seems that in the early spellings of children they do attempt to capture some of these elements. So size of letters, for instance, may be one means (used again, later, in adult forms such as in the bold letters of 'screamer' headlines) to indicate attitudinal meanings – meanings broadly in the area of 'importance', 'intensity', and so on. Example 2.2, pp 34–7 gives several such examples.

This is not to say that meaning elements that are of more conventional kinds, such as words, 'sayings' and phrases, are therefore necessarily unproblematic for a child to spell. If we take words to be the spellings of meanings, then a new problem arises. On the one hand, it is not at all clear what the boundaries of meanings are and how these boundaries are marked or recognized. On the other hand, it is not necessarily clear to the child what the meaning elements themselves are. On the face of it, the problem of spelling is discovering the correspondences between sounds and graphic elements, of sounds and letters. That is not a simple matter. In fact it is more complicated than that. Before they can do that, children need to know what the boundaries of the larger sound units such as words are, and to do that, they really need to know what the meaning elements are. If you know none of these, you really have a difficult task in prospect, literally the kind of job you do to get a PhD in Linguistics. On pp 38–9 and pp 40–1 there are two examples, 2.3 and 2.4, that illustrate this problem.

Let me give an example of a slightly different kind to illustrate what I mean. Some years ago, when we lived in Sydney, going home from work on the bus I used to see – and puzzle about – a sign on the exterior wall of a Lebanese restaurant in Newtown, an inner Sydney suburb. The sign read 'Your welcome to our mix plate and pizza'. This caption was displayed, in semicircular fashion, around a painted image showing what I took to be the 'mix plate and pizza'. What, I thought, had led to this spelling? Of course, I could have gone to experience 'my welcome', and tried the 'mix plate' in this restaurant; and I could have then engaged the owner in a conversation about his sign. And maybe he could have given me his account of how these spellings came about. However, I never did, and instead I kept on puzzling.

Example 2.1

Spelling the meaning of a letter

This *b* is an example of spelling as a visual matter, of **spelling as writing**. Barney has seen his name written many times, and has no doubt asked many times how his name is **written**. The initial letter will draw the child's attention for a number of reasons: it is first; whether written in capitals throughout or not, the *b* will always be large; and it is very likely that he has heard parents, carers or others say 'B is for Barney'.

Coming from his own position, in which objects, concepts, ideas are likely to have a representation as a picture, he may want to assume that *b* is a 'picture' of Barney, and therefore should have, recognizably, features of 'Barney'. The child's approach to making sense of letters is twofold: a **representation** is always in some important way a **likeness**; and in this case the likeness is that of the image of Barney. The child endows the letter with meaning, according to his logic. (Barney was 3 years old when he drew/wrote this *b*.)

(Continued on pages 32–33)

The drawing 'This is me' was done by Michael, and an example of his writing of his name is underneath (it comes from a separate page from that of the drawing, but it was written on the same day). I produce it here to show the 'closeness' of this child's representation of an image of himself and of the letters of his name. (Michael had just turned 5.)

Example 2.1 (continued)

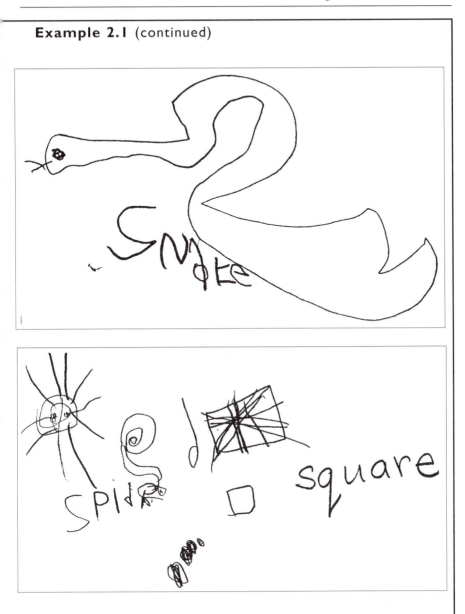

The 'S-snake', also done by Michael at this age, shows the same principle at work: endowing the letter with meaning by making it a picture of
a thing, the snake. The snake's tongue, clearly drawn, may be a parallel
attempt to endow the letter with the meaning of the sound made by the
hissing snake.

Example 2.2

The spelling of affect and emotion

Mutahara has spelled her name with exaggeratedly long letters. No doubt she is trying to achieve an aesthetic effect; at the same time the size of the letters signals just how important her name is, and how big she herself is.

(Continued on pages 36–37)

Example 2.2 (continued)

The many bars on the *E* at the beginning of Emily's writing of her name, seem, in their excessiveness, to signal exuberance and importance. This 'style' of *E* lasted for about six months in Emily's writing.

In the case of the drawing of a poster for Halloween, the comic-strip-like style to indicate terror and fright has been extended to the shaky form of the shapes of the letters: the quaking and shaking of terror is iconically represented in the shaky drawing of the letters.

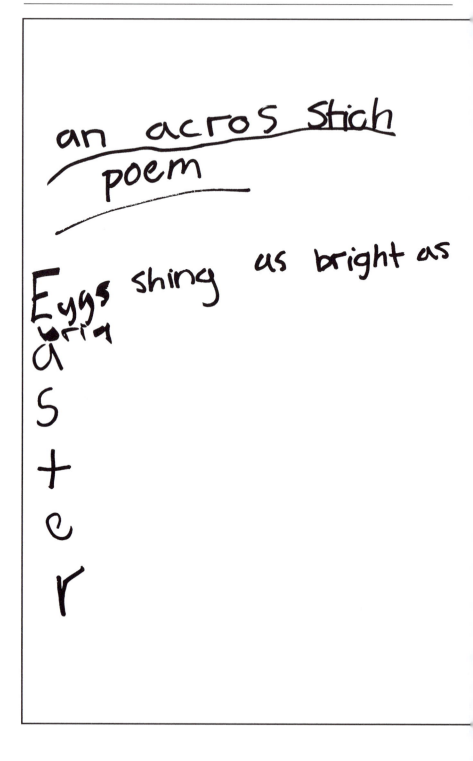

Example 2.3

What are the words I have to spell?

Emily had several attempts at making acrostic poems. This had been a concept introduced by her teacher in class. It seems that the word had been introduced in the teacher's talk (it is one of several 'concepts' brought in through the newly introduced Literacy Hour, a part of the British Government's *National Literacy Strategy*, formally introduced in 1998). The concept had obviously caught the child's imagination.

Her route to making sense of this sound sequence is via sound and grammar. I assume that this is the plausible way to go for her, because, she might argue for herself, 'This is a technical term', and as such not one she knows, so that, even though she does not know this word, this is not a conceptual difficulty for her; she knows that there are lots of words that she has not heard before. (The *acros* may relate in some way to the fact that you do move 'across', even if it is down the line of letters.)

Without a prior analysis, here of a fundamentally grammatical kind, spelling cannot be attempted. You need to know what it is you are asked to spell before you can spell it. The child has to make inferences about the grammatical structure of this sound shape, and from that she attempts a guess at the unknown word. What is clear is that spelling is intertwined with fundamental aspects of the larger language system: with grammar, syntax, and word knowledge.

Frogs born.

James

'When Frogs are born there called
Frogs born and there in littel rond bits of
jelly so they cont do nofing.

Tadpole + frog   E/2/97

I auready Knew that frog's have
Baby's.   I have learnt tath tadpole
come aut of frog's sporn. ✓
I allso learnt that thay they Brev uder
Water. hawever the mose
interesting thing was that
the tadpod. are the blak
spoes

Example 2.4

Spelling the meaning I

James clearly does not know the word *frogspawn*. His problem is to make sense of the sound sequence that he has heard, in several ways. The questions that he seems to have asked himself might have been: What **is** this word? What **are** these words? What is the **meaning** of this word/these words that I have heard?

His solution is to take meaning as his key. The context clearly suggests that this is about the reproductive processes of frogs: it is about how frogs are born.

To know what the words-as-sound-units are he clearly has to make a decision first about what the meaning is: that is, what the words-as-meaning-units are. Only then can he 'spell' this sound sequence, and in my view he spells it **accurately**. He has not made a spelling mistake with *Frogs born*. Spelling here is indistinguishable as an activity from thinking about vocabulary, grammar and meaning.

Notice with what meticulous care the frogspawn is drawn. James is very careful, and clearly takes real interest and pride in this task.

Spelling the meaning II

Emily clearly does not know the word *frogspawn*. Her problem is like James's: she has to make sense of a sound sequence she has heard; again she does this in several ways. The questions she seems to have asked are like James's questions, but her answers differ.

Her solution is to take sound as the key, and to say 'Ah, here is another word I don't know: a (technical) word for the stuff tadpoles come out of'. She also relies on grammatical knowledge, which tells her that structures of the kind **noun's noun** (*lion's mane; cat's tail*) are quite common, and obviously *frog's sporn* belongs to that group.

She has relied on an acute sense of hearing, in that quite frequently the joining of a word final *s* (frog's) with a following word initial *s* (sporn) leads to a pronunciation of a single *s*, *frogsporn*, even though in its spelling it has the two letters *s*. She has assumed that this is one such case, and therefore has the two letters *s*. Of course this demonstrates that she has learned – or deduced – such an abstract rule of pronunciation and spelling for herself.

In both examples, meaning provides the essential clue to grammatical structure, and therefore to words, therefore to sound shape, and therefore to the letter shape.

My explanation of his 'mix plate' has to do with my earlier point about the different phonetic substance of sounds such as *t* in different contexts. At the end of a word such as *mixed* two things happen phonetically. The *x* we know is pronounced as *ks*, a sequence of voiceless sounds (sounds made with no vibration of the vocal chords); and following these two voiceless consonant sounds the *t* is barely or not pronounced, especially when the plosive *t* is followed by the plosive *p* as it is at the start of *plate*, and certainly not in the working-class dialect of Sydney English. A sequence of consonants such as in *mikst* just takes too much effort to pronounce. When this consonant sequence is immediately followed by another two consonants, the *p* and *l* of plate, to produce a sequence of five consonants – kstpl – as in *mikstplait*, the articulation becomes difficult: try saying *kstpl*! So the owner, or his signwriting friend, simply transcribed what they actually heard, the sequence with the *t* left out, perfectly accurately and, of course, 'incorrectly' from the point of view of 'proper' spelling.

The children who wrote *a cross stich* and *Frog's born* had rather fewer linguistic and cultural resources to draw on than the owner of the Lebanese restaurant in inner Sydney, but actually proceeded in quite similar ways. The writer of *a cross stich* clearly did not know the meaning unit *acrostic* and had not met it either as a sound word or as a meaning unit. She therefore attempted a multiple analysis: first a grammatical analysis, which produced a (noun) **phrase** and its component 'words', *a cross sti(t)ch*; from that she produced a phonetic/phonological analysis, the transliteration by the letters a.c.r.o.s.s..s.t.i.c.h. The first analysis produces a transcription of the grammatical elements (the indefinite article *a*, the adjective *cross* and the noun *stich*): we can call it the 'grammatical spelling'. It also produces the transcription of the meaning elements, the spelling by words of the meaning, which we could call the 'semantic spelling': a stich which is cross. The second analysis produces the graphic spelling, the spelling by letters of the sounds. The problem with *Frog's born* and *Frogs sporn* is practically the same. Again, neither of the young spellers has a knowledge of the meaning units, the words. The first child uses his knowledge of the environment, namely the fact that this sound sequence has occurred in the context of a lesson on how frogs reproduce – 'ah, this is about how frogs are born', and from that he makes an inference about the meaning unit. His route is via meaning. The other child's strategy is to go via the route of sound. I assume that she might have thought 'I can hear two clear sound units, *frogs* and *sporn*; there must be a word *sporn* which I don't know; nothing unusual in that!'

Before I pass on, let me give one further example from my own experience. In a conversation, I happened to ask my interlocutor where she worked. I heard what I thought was 'the early learning foundation'. 'Oh,' I said, 'the early learning foundation.' 'No, the **urban** learning foundation.' Now, had the occasion required it, I might have written down 'place of work: early learning foundation'. I assume that if someone had read that, no one would have regarded 'early' as a misspelling of 'urban'. Why not? The answer would be that it was, simply, a mishearing. But why is it that, when a child (or a learner of a new language) mishears and records their mishearing, we think of it as misspelling? Of course, you might say that if I had heard the word properly I would have spelled it correctly; but so, we might say, would the children who recorded their hearings and find them treated as spelling problems. My strategy was exactly like theirs, or that of the restaurant owner: I attempted, first, to make sense of a segment of sound, then I gave it its word shape as meaning; and, after that, I could have (although I didn't) recorded that word shape in letters.

Maybe I am missing a fundamental point, for instance the fact that I know (and know how to spell) the word *urban*. But the processes that led me to hearing *early* are exactly like those that have led the child spellers, whose strategies I'd like to understand, to their spellings.

The Lebanese restaurant owner was dealing with a new language: one that is very different from his native Arabic. His problem is one that is shared by everyone who has to learn a new language, and has to learn to write and spell it. His problem is faced by all children learning to write and to spell. Loanwords might seem in this context to pose a particular problem. After all, words that 'belong' in the language at least share the sound system of that language. But words that are from another language and from an entirely different sound system – and in particular if they are recent borrowings, new arrivals – bring with them not just new meanings but also unknown sounds and sound combinations from that other language.

On pp. 44–51 I show some examples (2.5–2.8) of children's strategies in dealing with this problem.

Yet in a way I feel that it would be better to think about the case of loanwords as though it was the normal case. If we assumed that, for children who are learning to spell, every word is a loanword, then we might get a better sense of the real difficulties facing them. After all, they do not know, and cannot be expected to know, that *phone* is a borrowing from (Ancient) Greek. When a child spells *phone box* as *Fone box* she is simply responding to the sounds she hears with the logic of the English sound system.

She is also attempting – without knowing it of course – to engage in a bit of spelling reform, something that many eminent people before her have attempted and failed to do. (George Bernard Shaw's famous example of the spelling of *fish* as *ghoti* – if we took the *gh* as in *laugh*, the *o* as in *women*, and the *ti* as in *nation* – was his attempt to point out the need for reform.) Their failures were not due to the inherent problems in this matter, although that is how the issue is usually explained: 'English is so complex, no attempts to reform its spelling could succeed, or could do justice to the complexity (or subtlety) of our language'. The other objection posed equally frequently is 'loss of our heritage': if we were to spell *knight* as *nite*, or as *nait*, we would loose all that wonderful evidence of a rich linguistic and cultural history. I agree that that is so; because of my own interests in origins I actually like these vestiges of a rich past. I like the fact that the *sk* sequence as in *skirt* tells me about the centuries of Viking invasions and then settlement in many areas of England, in the 'Danelaw'; and I like knowing that *shirt*

1) Robabe yoget
2) Chem Fresh
3) Shozden ok Lamb
4) potatos
5) Crunchi pent butten
6) blanchd armens 250

Example 2.5

Loanwords 1: what is a loanword?

Loanwords pose fundamental questions, for a child as much as for a theory of spelling. They entirely undermine the regularities – such as they are – of the sound system of a language, and therefore undermine the regularities – such as they may be – of the relation between sequences of sounds and sequences of letters.

It is tempting to say that the first question for a child might be or ought to be 'What is a loanword?', so that she or he might proceed differentially with its spelling. But of course children do not know about the concept of loanwords, so in principle for them every word both is and is not a loanword, and is treated by the child-speller in the same way.

There are many further questions, though I'll mention just one here: 'When does a word cease to be a loanword?' In this first example here, this becomes a real question, say with the word *almonds*.

For my first two examples of loanwords, 2.5 and 2.6, I have chosen entirely ordinary and everyday texts, to show just how central this issue is.

To ask my first question: 'What is a loanword?' In this most ordinary of activities – making a shopping list (the example is a real one) – I would nominate *rhubarb, yoghurt, crème fraiche, potatoes, almonds,* and possibly *blanched.* The languages represented here, and with them their phonological systems, are Arabic (*rhubarb*), Bulgarian (*yoghurt*), French (*crème, fraiche, ?blanched*), and Spanish (*potatoes*).

To ask my second question: 'When does a word cease to be a loanword?' Do we still think of *rhubarb* or *almond* or *potato* as loanwords? Yet each of these three words presents a specific problem for spelling, which derives from their origin in the sound system of another language.

This child-speller has 'normalized' the spelling of these words, and has in effect turned them into 'English' words. And in this lies a further issue: the very existence of loanwords, their large number and their 'ordinariness', makes it completely normal for the child – or the flower vendor – to expect strangeness in spellings, and thereby to undermine the idea that spellings are 'regular' and predictable.

Blockbuster story

This is another entirely ordinary text, a story about an ordinary set of events (with the exception of the parents' absence). The same questions apply as before: are *allotment*, *video*, *Blockbusters* (the name of a video-rental shop, itself adopted from the concept of commercially successful Hollywood movies) loanwords, or are they 'English' words?

Monday 17th June

On sunday i went too the alotmit
and waen i cam hoeum i wocht
a vidyow from blokbistis and then
it was iftr 9 a clok So then
i had too go to bed but i mist
my mum and dad but then iwas
owkay

Example 2.6

Loanwords 2: making loanwords into 'English'

Normalizing difference: The class 'roll'

In the multicultural, multi-ethnic classrooms of contemporary cities, where knowledge of many languages is represented by the children in the school, difference is taken as normal by the children, and certainly so in the lower years of schooling. Differences in names are accepted as entirely usual; and the effects on spelling are, again, to make difference normal. This has its effects as much on 'English' names as on the names that originate in other than European cultures. Here are the names, in order, as best as I can establish them: James, Jake, Rorey, Rebekah, Orlando, Iona, David, [Samei:a], Adam, Rose, Emily, Daniel, Heather, Rachel, Shannon, Max, Antony, Joe, Mischa, Lola, Rowey, Jordan, Kashmere, Callum, Michael.

Jams ✓   30 in the clas
Jako ✓
rore,u ✓
Vebokah [h]
Or ba'dow ✓
Iona ✓
david ✓
Sirmá4ir ✓   hawe mony in to day
adим ✗   monday 4th of Juny
VoSe ✓   21
Emil4 ✓
danYob ✓
hevir ✓
Vachol ✓
Shan an ✓
max ✓
Atinel4 ✓
Joave ✓
Mishir ✓
LoLa ✓
Vowe4 ✓
Jodrin ✓
Cashmer ✓
Calim michael ✓

van goaths courlaves

Tonight
~~Tomotow~~   Dinner

Starter: Dips!
Zezreca & peater bread
Garot

Example 2.7

Loanwords 3: transforming the sound shape of loanwords into the sound shape of English

van Goaths courlures (van Gogh's colours)

This example illustrates the complex chain of reasoning that this child-speller seems to have employed in dealing with the problem posed by this loanword. The child heard, I expect, an *f* (the pronunciation of van Gogh's name adopted by most English speakers is with an *f*). But this child also knows that *f* sounds are often spelled as *th* – even though in many of her spellings she has gone 'in the other direction' and has transcribed the *th* as in *Maths* as *Mafs*. So the reasoning seems to be: I hear an *f* sound, but what I'm probably supposed to be hearing is a *th* sound (as in *think*). So I'll write it as *th*, as I expect I'm meant to do.

The *oa* instead of *ou* results from adopting an 'English' spelling strategy; *ou* would usually produce a long diphthong, as in *sound*, and not produce the short *o* sound that the child will have heard.

Dinner menu

I'm not sure what the 'official' spelling of *Tsatsiki* (the Middle Eastern yoghurt and cucumber dip) is; I have frequently seen the one I have adopted here, but I've also seen others. The child seems to have heard a pronunciation more *e* and *i* like than the one I would use, and consequently her spelling reflects what she has heard.

The sequence of sounds, whether the *ts* which occurs twice, or the sequence of consonants and vowels in the three syllables of the word *Tsa-tsi-ki,* makes for a syllable structure that is 'un-English' (a sequence of consonant (c) and vowel (v) three times in succession: cv-cv-cv), and so the child-speller adopts a more English-like syllable structure: *zez-ke-a* (to put it somewhat abstractly, not cv-cv-cv, but cvc-cv-v), both in look and sound.

In other words, we might say that what the child-speller has done is to transcribe the vowel 'colours' that she has heard accurately, but she has fitted them or transformed them into the syllable structures of English.

With the word *pitta* the problem seems, and perhaps is, simpler: the vowel colours are readily reproduced, and the syllable structure of the loanword (which, in the original, may be like that of *Tsa-tsi-ki* , i.e. cv-cv, *pi-ta*) fits more readily with the look and the sound of English syllables: *peat-er,* or *pit-ta.*

Example 2.8

Loanwords 4: the truly strange, and the entirely familiar

(a) Credit Agricole

With all of the preceding examples, the child was dealing with words that she or he had heard many times, in ordinary contexts of use, and spelled in 'their own' language. With this example, the child is dealing with the spelling of a strange word in a strange language. The writing of the word, and the drawing of the bank's logo, occurred in the context of a game of playing 'Banks', in France.

It seems clear to me that the strangeness of the whole larger social, cultural and linguistic context has meant that the child has far fewer resources with which to approach this problem, and the spelling of the word is, as a consequence, a quite tentative approximation only, not as confident at all as her spellings of the preceding examples.

(b) Fone box

As my last example of loanwords here, a spelling where it seems clear that the child's answer to the question 'When does a word cease to be a loanword?' is 'When its sound sequences, and the sound–letter relations, have become entirely like those of the borrowing language'. This word is, in my view, in no sense a loanword any longer. It has become English, and it is spelled by the child as an English word; it is transcribed accurately, but predictably – thanks to the efforts of grammarians, phonologists, 'purists', pedants and others – spelled incorrectly.

is the spelling of the 'same' word, but is the vestige of the earlier Germanic invasions. But the price, in each case, is paid in the problems faced by young and often not so young spellers. I'm not so confident that my antiquarian interests are worth that cost.

2.2 Visible language

So far I have proceeded on the assumption that if we think of language as sound, then to spell is to put sound into graphic form via the means of letters. This assumption has become commonsense, 'natural', in cultures using alphabetic means of recording their languages. Such assumptions are neither commonsense nor natural in 'literate cultures' that do not use the alphabet. In alphabetic cultures we are used to thinking that the alphabet is a unique achievement, marking the highest form of cultural and intellectual development in the recording of language in human history. Yet many languages, now as in the past, make or made use of non-alphabetic forms of writing. Hieroglyphics are a well-known example in the cultural histories of Mediterranean, Middle Eastern and European cultures. In fact the alphabet itself is a development from the picture-writing of hieroglyphs. Other cultures had chosen to move similarly in the directions of picture-writing, whether the cultures of central America or the cultures of East Asia. If in alphabetical cultures the transcriptional system records sounds, in picture-writing cultures the transcriptional systems record not sounds but ideas or concepts or words as concepts – hence the names ideographic, pictographic, logographic.

The question that nags at me, as difficult as it is to get at, is: What is the commonsense around language and writing that people from cultures with these pictorial recording systems have developed? My hunch, difficult to prove, is that for 'us' the alphabet leads us to think as the first step that 'language is sound expressed by letters'; and only at the second step that 'sound expresses meaning'. For users of ideographic languages, the first step might be 'language is ideas or "concepts" (expressed as visual entities)', and the second step is that 'ideas are communicated in speech, by sounds'. Of course, even if something like this were correct, it would be a huge oversimplification: 4000 years or so of the use of, say, the Chinese writing system has led to many complex developments: so that some of the characters have grammatical function, some have the purely phonological function of indicating sound features, and others, the majority, have the function of expressing ideas.

Once we have grasped this deep distinction between these different writing systems, it allows us to look again at our own situation, that of the roman version of alphabetic writing. Two obvious points can be made on the basis of this new understanding. One: even alphabetic writing is a visual medium, and therefore it can be and is treated as a kind of picture. Two: many practices in the teaching of writing – spelling included – base themselves precisely on that very idea, namely the recognition of words as visual entities, as 'visible language'.

In both cases we encounter the same problem as before: What is it that is being spelled? In pictographic cultures what is spelled is ideas as pictures; in alphabetic cultures what is spelled is sounds as pictures. Yet in many (first or second) language-teaching programmes, word recognition plays an important part. For instance, the teacher may hold up a card on which the word *baker* is written, and the children are asked to say the word. This method is most often supplemented by a picture of the object also on the card – a picture of the baker, or of the cat, the horse, etc. The method conflates at least two distinct matters. One is the written word (or the written word plus the image of the object) as a 'spelling' of the idea: the printed word *baker* as the spelling of the idea BAKER. This is a version of the deeply entrenched idea that 'words are the names of things'. The other is the matter of the written word as an entity made up of a sequence of smaller things, letters, with which a whole sound-complex is associated. It is clear that a teacher can introduce any number of variations into this scheme. For instance, she can focus on the fact that the printed entity is made up of smaller printed entities; or she can focus on the sounding of the smaller entities, the letters. Or she can focus on the 'meaning-end' of the structure, and explore the relation between printed word and image, or between the image and the object in the world. It is neither a particular secret nor a surprise that teachers do all of these, in response to the perceived needs of the learners, to help structure their experience and their learning paths.

To this must be added the long prior experience of print by children, whether as story, as the child's printed name, as advertising or as logo, on the television or in the street. So, whichever of these teaching methods children encounter in school, for them as for adults spelling is also an engagement with an important part of the visible world. Spelling can be the drawing of the discrete elements of the written/printed word – the drawing of letters as pictures – or spelling can be the drawing of ideas, as whole words. Spelling at early stages is also the drawing of the picture of the dog, the cat or the baker. Usually it is likely to be all of these, in different ways, depending on the child's interest at a particular moment. The early spellings of children combine the two routes that human cultures have taken: spelling of ideas as pictures, and spelling of sounds as pictures. In the contrast of these two routes it is clear that spelling of sound as pictures has real problems: letters are simply not very good or convincing pictures of sounds – hence the 's is for snake' examples of alphabet charts.

Spelling – as the drawing of the visible world of print, and of writing – is to reproduce a part of the visible world, either as a real image or as a kind of image, by means of a system of visible marks. Spelling as drawing allows the child to stay in the same medium, broadly speaking: reproducing a picture (of a letter, or a sequence of letters) as a picture. This is also how children come into graphic ways of making meaning, from their initial exuberantly expressive circular 'scribbles', to the later, much more reflective drawing of writing (see Example 2.9, pp 54–55).

This approach is a far remove from seeing spelling merely as the transcription or transduction of sound into graphic form. With spelling as the drawing of an

Example 2.9

Spelling meaning as image

As I have suggested, one commonsense view of spelling is that it is making visible marks to 'stand for' audible marks, for sounds. This 'stand for' relation is a translation of the sound meaning into the graphic meaning. The idea of 'sound meaning' may be difficult to grasp: it is not 'the meaning associated with a sound, or sounds' (i.e. *c-a-t* means 'cat') but the meaning, the colour, the texture of a sound (a meaning such as: the *a* in c-a-t is a 'short', 'flat' sound, while the *u* as in b-oo-t is a 'long', 'round', 'full' sound).

This view makes spelling into the transcription of kinds of meaning, a translation of meaning in one medium into meaning in another medium. We can use this as a broad, general definition: for example, someone who gestures behind a speaker's back may be translating the meaning 'pomposity' from the speaker's **talk** into exaggerated, bizarre **gestures**. In this view the first set of marks in this example might be the 'spelling' of 'it goes round and round, energetically, in a really fast fashion'. Gradually, over time (the first three set of marks were made roughly at intervals of six months), more meaning is expressed: in the process the initial meaning is not lost, but becomes overlaid with more and other meanings.

By the time that this child drew the circles, at the age of 3 (each on a separate sheet), the initial meanings have receded somewhat, and the idea not just of 'circularity' but of 'circle' is fully present. But the initial meanings of 'it goes round and round, . . .' are still there, and they make it easy to move from the 'spelling' of 'circularity' and 'circle', to using several circles to spell wheels, which do go 'round and round', and to use several circles to spell 'car', which is what the final set of marks 'spell': 'this is a car'.

This route to spelling, the spelling of meaning by image, is one that many cultures have taken, at different points in human history, from the cultures of Central America (Mayan, Aztec) to cultures of the Mediterranean, of Africa, of East Asia and Australia.

image (whether of a real object, or of a letter, or of a line of print), the relation between the thing to be drawn and the thing drawn will seem clear to the child, even if her or his efforts may not seem adequate to the eye of the adult. That fact is hugely important. When the child draws (or 'writes') the wooden model of the dinosaur that is standing on the chimney breast in her room, it is clear to her that there is a direct relation between the model and her drawing. When she draws a line of print the relation will seem equally clear to her. But with spelling as the drawing of sound, the relationship between the characteristics of the sound and the characteristics of the drawing of the letter are far from clear; or – to put it as strongly as it needs to be put – the relationship is actually impossible to establish. That is why alphabet charts try so hard to make that relation seem plausible (the hissing of the snake, plus the shape of the snake as the motivation for the shape of the letter *S*). In reality there is simply no plausible relation between the shape of a letter and the often many different sounds that the letter is used to 'spell'. Sound and graphic shape are unrelated. Object and drawing **are** related. Drawing ideas is in accord with the principles of the child's approach; drawing sounds is not. This is one major source of problems in the learning of writing, and in spelling.

In any case, what is clear is that children encounter spelling in at least these two modes – as the transduction of sound into graphic form, and as the reproduction of a graphic form (letters as a kind of image) with a graphic form. Spelling is, among other things, a matter of dealing with the visible/visual world. In this guise, the problems of spelling are different. Now it is not the problem of explaining (away) the oddities of the relation of language as sound to language as visible marks (say, the rule 'the *e* on the end of the word lengthens the (vowel) sound that comes before', or however this is expressed). The issue now is to know and learn which features of the visible world represented in an image or an image-like thing are central and which are not.

This might seem entirely straightforward: a letter, after all, is a letter; and the shapes are clear enough. I want to show how very complex this whole area actually is. Anyone who has tried or has had to try to deal with a strange script – Arabic, Cyrillic, etc. – will know how uncertain one suddenly becomes about this very simple question: is this squiggle, or this fatter bit, or this blob essential or is it merely a matter of 'style'? Lest it be thought that the elephant is labouring to bring forth a mouse, let me start by quoting from a recent document published by the Teacher Training Agency (the TTA), a quasi-governmental body given authority to 'oversee' the 'training' of teachers in England. Example 2.10 comes from a small booklet that focuses on matters of grammar and spelling, and is issued as advice to teachers. The point at issue is a seemingly slight one, though its consequences are anything but slight. It turns, in my view, precisely on a recognition and acknowledgement of spelling as a matter of drawing an aspect of the visible world.

Of course, this example is also a clear illustration of the implicitly held commonsense that spelling is the transduction of speech to writing: that is the basis for the assumption that this young speller has an **auditory** difficulty. In the booklet we are given the example in printed form. This obliterates, obviously, any trace of the child's **drawing**, of any evidence of his attempt to make sense of the visible world in visible form. Without a clear sense that spelling is a mater of visual recording, we cannot hope to deal with an issue such as that in Example 2.10.

If we want to discover and understand the complexity involved in making sense of the *visible* world we have to be prepared to look with fresh eyes, and to look at things we have been taught to overlook. My next example attempts to show what I mean; it may seem very slight. It concerns the attempt by a 3-year-old to write a thank-you note to one of her friends. The 3-year-old happened to be my daughter, 'doing her work' while I was doing mine, on the floor of my study, at home. She had gotten up from her work and asked me to write 'thank you' on a piece of paper. Example 2.11 on pp 60–61 reproduces my scribbled 'thank you' and her copy of the model provided by me.

If this suggests the kinds of thinking processes involved for this child, and the kinds of new looking involved for us, then my next set of examples is meant to show what kinds and what range of factors actually have to be recognized and understood by a child – and therefore by us – in the business of visual spelling. It may be that all of these things are known to every reader of this book, or to everyone involved in research into early writing, or involved with the teaching of teachers around these questions. Nevertheless it may still be useful to show the painstaking, meticulously rigorous, gradual process of analysis on which visual spelling is founded. My examples (2.12–2.14) show the process that one child has engaged in, over a period of just over one year, between the ages of 3 years 10 months and 5 years and 2 months, in the spelling of her name.

So far I haven't asked the question about a young speller's recognition of the word as a whole unit, although the Emily example lends some support to a view that as well as attending to the individual graphic elements, children keep in mind the overall 'shape' of the word as a visual unit. Why else, after all, would Emily twice have written her name as in example 2.13?

A further factor emerges here, to which I shall return in some of the later chapters: the matter of what I shall call, I hope not too grandly, aesthetics. The **look** of writing as something beautiful, the use of writing as a matter of asserting one's individual style, certainly enters into visual aspects of spelling. This appears as much in individual letter shapes, and in the styles which young writers develop in their writing/drawing of letters, for quite often long periods, as it does in the spelling of whole words or lines or texts (Example 2.15).

Of course this could be regarded as hardly being a matter of spelling, but rather as being a question of handwriting. Maybe it is best to be aware that the boundaries between what we or others decide to call spelling, and matters such as handwriting, grammar, and punctuation, are not hard and fast at all. They reflect our sense at a particular time of what this thing spelling is, more than they reflect settled and certain truths. In that way we are more likely to keep ears, eyes, and minds open wide.

Example 2.10

Spelling: the many meanings of a letter

A set of booklets *Assessing Your Needs in Literacy: Diagnostic feedback* published by the Teacher Training Authority (a semi-governmental agency established to have oversight of all aspects of the training of teachers in England) deals, among other issues, with those of the multifaceted problems of spelling. It is designed for teachers of children between the ages (roughly) of 8 and 11 years (Key Stage Two in the English National Curriculum). The materials recognize the wide variety of issues and their complexity, and

ii)   The following lists show the correct spellings and some of the pupil's miscues. Describe the nature of each of the misspellings. You may wish to use the previous categories.

Word	As in text	Nature of the misspelling
storm	stom	
when	wene	
terrible	terbul	
boat	bot	
cracked	crahct	
felt	felp	
cold	celd	
faded	fatid	
out	owt/late/aret	
last	loust	
dreams	drems	
another	anov	
came	game	
again	agen	
stayed	stad	
decided	desidid	
my house	miyis	

yet, in the end, fall into some of the errors of the commonsense views of spelling, with potentially serious consequences.

A page, reproduced here, shows a range of problems, and suggests possible accounts of the problems. This booklet does not provide a copy of the initial *handwritten* text, so we as readers cannot judge to what extent the printed text actually reproduces the visual/graphic characteristics of the child's writing. So we have no possibility of gaining a sense of the *visuality* of the child's writing, or of his or her sense of the visuality of spelling, of letters as images.

Let me give one example where this might matter: the instance of *felt/felp*. There are several things that could be said here. For instance, in the case of *faded/fatid* the comment is 'written as spoken'. My first question would be: 'Why could not *felp* be treated as an accurate attempt at spelling of what the child said or heard? In many dialects of English, *t* in the middle or at the end of a word becomes a 'glottal stop' (as in East or North London pronunciation of *better*: be/er, or, phonetically, [beʔə]. Glottal stops can replace *p* as well as *t;* or, to put it the other way round, starting from sound, from what the child heard or said a glottal stop can be translated into either the letter *t* or the letter *p*. If we take that route of explanation, then this is an accurate transcription of what the child heard.

There are other accounts, which are equally well founded or likely. They would also provide explanations for *cold/celd, last/loust, came/game*, and explanations that do not immediately invoke the dangerous label of 'auditory discrimination problem'.

One other alternative explanation is that the child had heard the *t* of *felt* as a *d*, which again is an entirely usual pronunciation. Word-final consonants, especially plosive consonants such as *t* or *p*, are often not pronounced: they 'get swallowed', or are barely pronounced, say as a *d*. In that case what may be involved may be nothing more or other than the question of the spatial orientation of the letter *d*. *d* and *p* have the same shape, but have a specific spatial orientation: *d* is *p* rotated by 180°. That is a very common feature of children's early writing/drawing of letters: and it has nothing at all to do with 'auditory discrimination problems'. If there is a 'problem' it is a visual/spatial one. Of course it is important that a child learns to draw the letter *d* correctly oriented, spatially. But perhaps it is even more important that those who are responsible for equipping (those who train) those who teach writing with subtle, complex, and not necessarily commonsense understandings, rather than jumping immediately to the diagnosis of a pathology.

Spelling as a matter of the visual, spelling as drawing – with all its characteristics, such as the use of space, of shape, of spatial orientation – might be involved in the *cold/celd*, and the *came/game* diagnoses as well.

Example 2.11

Spelling as visual meaning-making: a child's principles

In this example I continue to explore the matter of the visuality of spelling, and I also want to begin an exploration of a child-speller's reasoning – an exploration of the logic of making meaning of the world of writing.

The context for this 'spelling' was that Emily (then 3) and I were both 'doing our work' in my study – she on the floor, I at my desk. She was engaged in making a thank-you card for a friend, and she asked me how to write 'thank you'. I wrote the words on the paper she had been using. She went back to 'her work' and within a minute or so came back excitedly, saying 'Look, I've done it'.

What had she done? And what were the principles she had employed? Clearly, reading and then writing, for her, were a matter of discerning what the visual, graphic elements were: and as she did not know what (the) letters were, she had to use principles of deduction to establish what the constituent elements might be. My sense of this is (a) that she took this to be a matter of the visual world, of drawing, of the world of the graphic – in other words, sound was not an issue; and (b) that she applied the principle that 'things (in this case the 'lines' of the letter shape) that are connected belong together'; and that is how she arrived at the new letter that she produced.

This example might seem slight; to me it is profound in its implications. First, early writing, early spelling, is a matter of understanding a part of the visual world, and of understanding what the component elements of that world are; writing then is a matter of drawing, and of drawing meaning. Second, the child's attempt at visual spelling proceeds on the basis of entirely rational principles; the fact that this may be a rationality that differs from that of convention, or from that of adults, is of course another matter.

And I would certainly not be tempted to speak of 'visual discriminatory problems'. For me the task is to attempt to understand a different set of principles, and a different logic. From the basis of that understanding I might then be able to think about teaching this child about adult logic, and social convention.

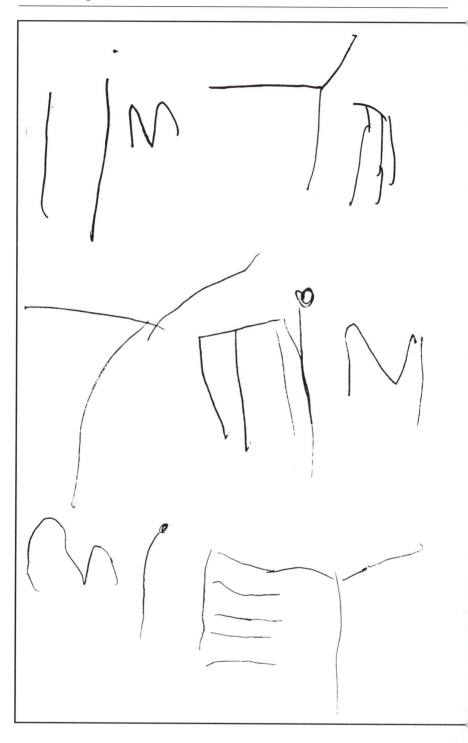

Example 2.12

The complexities of visual spelling

In this sequence of examples I explore the question of visual spelling in some detail. I draw attention to the multiplicity of factors involved in what seems, on the face of it, a relatively simple matter, namely that of copying (strings of) letters.

The three versions of Emily's spelling of her name were done at roughly the same time, in the three weeks following her fourth birthday. The questions that obviously arise for her are: How many discrete elements are there in my name? What are they? What is their shape? What is their spatial orientation? In two of the examples there are four 'letters'; in one there are five. In the examples with four letters, the visually least distinctive letter *l* is absent.

The third question, 'What is their shape?', obviously occupies the child. Again, the visually distinctive *M* seems not to present a real problem; and the dot on the *i* seems to make it distinctive. However, the *Y* and the *E* present a difficulty in terms of the spatial orientation of the letters, and in terms of the number of bars. The answer Emily seems to have adopted in relation to that question, 'How many bars?', is 'many'; where 'many' is always three or more. In all the examples I have there is no instance of an *E* with fewer than three and none with more than six bars. Clearly the child recognizes a distinction of 'three, and more than three', which seems to be roughly equivalent to 'many'; and a distinction between 'less than three, and more than six', where 'more than six' may mean 'very many'. In other words, in terms of letter shapes, she has decided that an E has 'many' bars; and the exact number that she draws at any one time may be a matter of affect: enthusiasm, exuberance, intensity – perhaps a mixture of the affective and of the aesthetic.

The fact that *E* is the first letter of her name may be a further reason for the exuberance displayed with the bars on the letter. However, **'first-ness'** and **sequence/order** in general do not seem to be an issue or a question for the child at this stage.

Example 2.13

The word as visual image

In this example (produced in the month after the previous ones) the dominant issue seems to be that of the order of the letters; the stability of the overall shape of the name; a kind of stylistic/aesthetic effect achieved by the 'framing' of the name with an initial and a final *E*.

The number of bars ranges between four and six. The matter of the spatial orientation of the *E* has been settled; and the arms on the *y* have a more consistent angle.

What is noticeable here, in relation to later versions, is that sequence is fixed; that writing direction is left to right; and that the directionality of the letters seems also to be fixed as left to right, though this is really only apparent with the *E*. In versions of the name written over the next few months all these become issues that are re-opened, explored and then settled. But above all, the name is here treated nearly as a logo, with the letter *E* (perhaps **the** important letter) framing the name at beginning and end.

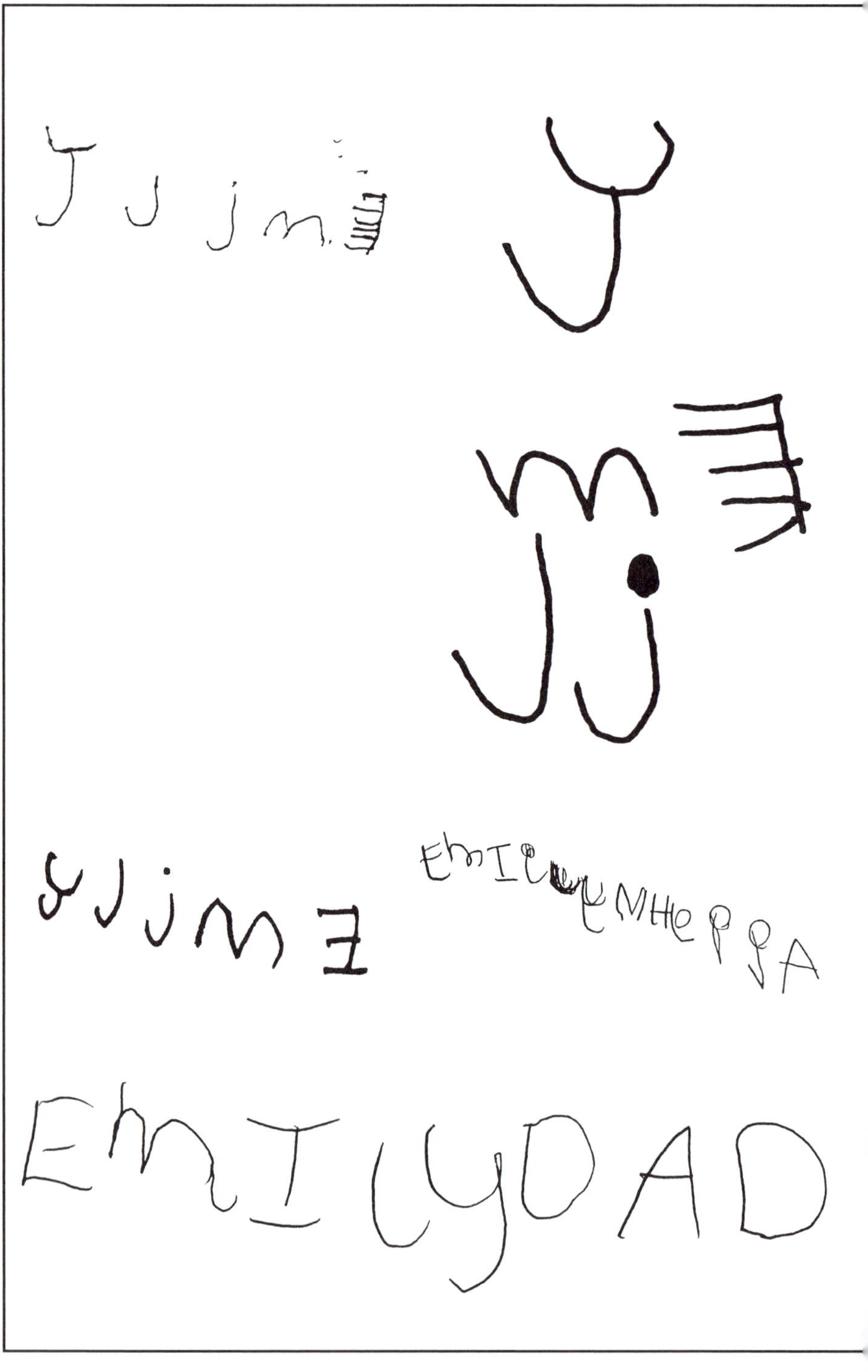

Example 2.14

Hidden principles of visual spelling

The first example, written in March 1994, three months after Example 2.13, shows the sudden decision by the child-writer to reverse the writing direction. In some way and for some reason or other **directionality** has become an issue. With the reversal of writing direction from right to left also comes the question of the directionality of the individual letters. In other words, **directionality** as a general issue rules both writing direction and the orientation of the shape of individual letters: it exists for the child as an abstract concept, which the child uses as a general means of understanding one aspect of writing.

The second example (May 1994) shows two things: the abstractness of the concepts of **directionality** and of **sequence**. The name and the letters are written from right to left. Because there was a drawing to the left of where the name appeared, Emily could not write the name on a single line, so she first wrote the *Em*, then the *il* (but with the hook on both *i* and *l* pointing to the left), and then, above the *Em*, the final *y*. In other words, the sequence of letters is strictly preserved; and it is a separate issue from directionality. (This will appear later, when I discuss *ordering* in a later Chapter 5.) But this example also shows that **linearity**, the order of letters on a *line*, is a separate issue from both directionality and sequentiality.

In the third example (July 1994) letter shapes appear to be settled, including that of *E*. However, the hook on the *y* goes in the same direction as do the hooks on the *l* and the *i*, showing that the general idea of right to left directionality overrides the demands of the shapes of the individual letters. By October 1994, the fourth example, the writing direction is reversed again, back to left to right. But, as in July, the child seems to go by a rule, something like 'whatever direction I write in, everything goes in the same direction!' Here the hook on the *y* goes in the same direction as the hook on the *i*, and as the writing direction.

By November, the fifth example here, this issue is now worked out. The child has realized that the directionality of the letters is a separate matter from the writing direction: the hooks on the *m*, the *l* and the *y*, go in different directions, correctly. On the same page Emily had written the sequence of numbers from 1–10 with a 6 'the wrong way round'; and this demonstrates that the principle of directionality is worked out separately for writing and letters, and for other sequences and for the orientation of numbers.

The principles that I have drawn out of the discussion of these examples are stable; they hold firm at the period when the child holds to them, and that period can be quite extended. In other words, there is no whim or wilfulness, no accident, no arbitrariness; no 'oh, she is just doing what comes into her head'. The principles are so firm that it is possible to date an example of the child's visual spelling with a high degree of precision, once the principles are understood.

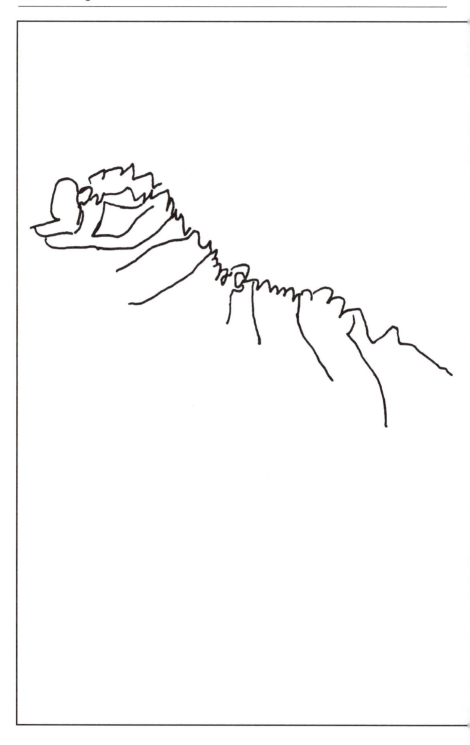

Example 2.15

Writing as drawing, drawing as writing: Tyrannosaurus rex

Alphabetic cultures have made the decision to treat the 'writing down of language' as a matter of writing down the **sounds** of the language with the **letters** of an alphabet. Cultures with ideographic (or pictographic, hieroglyphic, etc.) scripts have made the decision to treat the 'writing down of language' as a matter of writing down the **ideas** of the language with (conventionalized) **images**. This route may be the more plausible one for children.

In this example the child has 'written down', has 'spelled', the wooden model of a *Tyrannosaurus rex* standing on the mantelpiece in her room. She has spelled the features of the model in great and careful detail.

The second example on the facing page shows what I regard as the (same child's) drawing of (a line-and-a-half) of print, at much the same age. At this stage (at the age of 3) **drawing the world** and **writing the world** are much the same for a child: both are recordings, transcriptions, translations, 'spellings' of aspects of the world of the child.

The third example shows the drawing of writing by a child who lives in a pictographic/ideographic culture. For this 3-year-old, writing and drawing **are** the same, in many quite fundamental ways – from the physical action of drawing ideographs to the (more abstract) notion of language-as-image – and this link of idea and image will remain constant, even though it will become vastly more complex as she moves into her culture.

Objects and the drawings of objects are related. One mimics the other; one is an icon of the other. Sounds and the drawings of the shape of letters are unrelated; an *e* is not an icon of the sound /e/. The former accords with the child's principles of how meaning is recorded; the latter does not. Alphabetic cultures demand that children change tack from their route which relates idea with image, which is plausible to them, to the route of the alphabet, which relates sound with image (the image of a letter), which is not plausible to them, at least not initially. Many of the problems with spelling and writing may stem from that demand to change direction in such a fundamental way.

2.3 Standard language, dialects and spelling

Some years ago, when I was beginning to think about the linguistic/grammatical relations of speech and writing, I became marginally involved in the case of a 5-year-old who had been referred by his school to a speech therapist at the local hospital. In reading the speech therapist's transcript, I was struck by the possibility that it might have reflected the distance between his local dialect (Norwich) and that of standard English, at least as much as it reflected a speech impairment of some kind. I was able to borrow the original tape; my own attempt at transcription also appears in Example 2.16. In my transcript I tried to 'factor in' the features of Norwich dialect, and produced a written-down version, which resembled his own speech in his own dialect.

It seemed to me at that time that the child might well have had some problems in speaking, but that these problems were nowhere near as large, or of the kind as those that were implied in the speech therapist's transcript. Her record ignored, I felt, both the variations of the sound system of the local dialect and its distance from that of standard English, and had also ignored the differences in syntax and grammar between these two forms of English. In fact her record pathologized Norwich English, though the subject of her analysis was, of course, a child **speaker** of Norwich English.

Children, as I hope to demonstrate throughout the book, are relentlessly accurate phoneticians: they analyse sound with the acuity of young ears, not burdened with the habits of knowing what is proper, expected, or good, nor burdened with the grooved habits of the fully acquired sound system of a language. That is one reason why they have such facility in learning languages so easily and so well. They have neither a settled knowledge nor a particular investment in the systematicness of the sound system of the dialects spoken in their environments or of the standard language(s) in their society. Consequently they are able to record happily, easily, and very precisely what they actually hear, rather than what we think they should be hearing. Their spellings are the result of careful and unbiased acoustic analysis and transcription. This realization is one of the bases of any real understanding of the logic of children's spelling. However, the environments in which most children now live are hugely diverse, linguistically. Children come into contact with a multiplicity of dialects of English, whether local/geographical (North London, Yorkshire, Welsh English, East Anglian), or the dialects (and versions of English) of different social groups, or of any number of ethnically differing groups – the Englishes of the Indian subcontinent, of West Africa, of the Carribean, often all in their immediate neighbourhood and school – as well as the many versions of English as a global language that they hear on television.

Among these, inevitably, several dialects stand out prominently, for each child: the family's form(s) of English (or the family's main language); the language of the school; but also the language of the school playground; the gendered differences in forms of language use; and the languages of the peer groups in the locality. These are the materials available to any one child, out of which she or he has to fashion their sense of what English is, and on which they inevitably draw in trying to spell the words and phrases of English. This rich mix of English is the stuff that they have to 'spell'. Given children's precision in their recording and transcription of the sounds of language, then the greater the variety of spoken forms of English with which they are in contact, the greater the differences of spelling that they might produce. It is a great irony that these real and important abilities become reasons for their performing badly in terms of assessments in institutionalized education.

Clearly, social class enters into this. Given the relatively greater proximity of the spoken standard form of English to that of the written form, it is clear that children from families in which a form of standard English is in normal use have an automatic and often unacknowledged advantage in spelling compared with children whose families use varieties of English that are (more) remote from the standard.

2.4 A very brief history of the English language: the illogicality of spelling

Once a culture has developed, or borrowed, or achieved a writing system, or – equally frequently – has had one imposed by someone from outside, language can take two routes: once as speech and once as writing. From that moment on it is difficult to speak of 'English' or of 'French', because speech and writing in English or in French will develop in their own distinct ways, impelled and shaped by the distinct social environments in which they most typically occur. From then on we have 'written English' and 'spoken English', and the two go their own ways in many respects. Of course, many of the same people speak English as write English, and so the two forms of the language do not drift apart entirely. In fact there is constant interaction, with writing-like forms appearing in speech, and speech-like forms finding their way into writing. But to get a flavour of the distance that can separate them try reading this example of written English out aloud.

> Recommendation
> That reading resource teachers be encouraged to maintain comprehensive records of students' achievement levels including results on group-administered standardized tests, and that the results from individually administered standardized tests be used to inform decisions about whether a child is ready to return to normal classes.
> > *Weak readers in secondary schools.* (Discussion Paper No 17,
> > Education Department of Western Australia, 1987, p.14)

When I read this I run out of breath before I get to the end of sentences – and I have real difficulty trying to get the 'rhythm' or the 'feel' of it. Written English

Flawase

I Pike the Flawase
From my gadin i tone areawd
and Stop to See the

Yelow rose I go to Pike wine
a thone gest Stik in my figir

Example 2.16

Aesthetics: spelling something beautiful

The young poet has clearly taken great care with the visual presentation of the poem, both with the drawings and with the written text. Do we treat this as irrelevant? If not, what do we say?

If form is meaning, then the form of the writing and of the drawing here points to a meaning around 'I want this to be beautiful'. In fact, this speller uses an absolutely recognisable style when she is producing 'beautiful texts'.

Of course, we could say that this is a matter of handwriting; but it is not the child's usual handwriting, it is used only in these contexts. The fact that the spelling of the sound also points to 'heightened style' (a kind of sound exaggeration in a certain tonal and rhythmic direction) makes me regard this as being part of spelling, as the representation of particular kinds of meaning through the means of spelling as a visual medium.

is meant to be read with the eyes, and only some written English is meant to be read out loud, with lips and vocal chords working.

This separation of the two forms of the language introduces one problem for spelling, because spelling as 'sound put into letters' really assumes an identity between the spoken and the written forms of language, or rather it assumes that there is really only spoken language, which can however be 'caught' and 'captured' by some visible, graphic means. But writing in its most writing-like form no longer really has a spoken equivalent: it exists as a form of communication that is pretty well independent of speech. That is one, **real**, problem. There is a second problem, which is that this separation makes the emergence of a standard language so much easier, so much more likely; and over time the written form as the standard language comes to be seen as **the** language, whether as speech or as writing. Where before spelling was putting the sounds of speech into letters, now the boot is on the other foot, and the spoken version has to be fitted to the written. Where before sounding preceded spelling, now spelling dictates what sounding should be like. The many different varieties of English, whether of geographical or of social dialects, have to be fitted, however uneasily and awkwardly, to the unyielding norms of the standard language. That fitting has to be achieved by all young spellers for themselves; and clearly it helps if you happen to grow up speaking a form of English that is closer to rather than more distant from the standard form.

That is a real problem, and it isn't made any easier by the fact that society by and large doesn't see the problem. But this is a problem faced by all beginning writers in all alphabetic cultures – in their different ways. English spelling, however, is much more tricky than spelling in some other (particularly European) languages – say Spanish, or Italian, or even German for instance. And the reason for that is the truly chequered history of the English language. This is not the place for a detailed history, but it may be useful to give even quite a brief sketch to show how English spelling cannot be understood as a coherent, consistent, 'logical' system of transcribing sound to letters. It is by and large a mixture of two such systems: that of a Romance language, Norman (and then Angevin) French, and that of a Germanic language, or better, the varieties of Germanic languages spoken along the North Sea coasts of what are now Denmark and Germany some 2000 years ago. The people speaking these Germanic languages (the Angles, the Jutes, and the 'Saxons') arrived some time in the fifth century (the year given in Bede's Anglo-Saxon chronicle is 449), initially as allies invited in to defend post-Roman Britain against marauding groups of people from just a bit further north, from the seaboards of what are now Norway and southern Sweden, the Vikings. They soon 'settled', and founded the seven early English kingdoms: Kent, Mercia, Northumbria, East Anglia, Essex, Wessex, and Sussex. Given that these people arrived speaking distinctly different – though mutually intelligible – forms of language meant that from the very beginning there wasn't a single English language: there were quite distinct dialects. This is salutary to bear in mind: the dialect of the Northumbrians – those who settled north of the Humber – has as ancient a heritage as the dialect of those who settled in the southern parts of England, later to become, largely for political and economic reasons, the 'standard' form of (English) English.

The later settlement of the Vikings in the eastern parts of England, in what became known as the Danelaw, (though also in other regions right around the coast of England) during the ninth and tenth centuries led to a first significant addition of a distinctively different sound system. This brought the *shirt–skirt* distinction already mentioned, along with many others – often preserved in place names such as the *-thorp(e)*, *-by*, and the *fell*, *beck*, *garth* of northern English usages. The arrival, after the battle of Hastings, of Norman French was a more significant event, linguistically as well as socially. It brought the sound system of a distinctly different member of the Indo-European group of languages, a Romance language (derived from Latin and related closely to Italian, Spanish, Portuguese, Provençal, etc.) in contrast to the Germanic languages (related languages such as Dutch, German, Danish, Swedish) already present in England.

But this event also introduced a vast political and social distinction, the repercussions of which are with us to the present day. In effect the new rulers, the new upper classes, used French, and those who were ruled used the local, Germanic language. This difference can be seen to persist into the present: formal English usage is largely 'latinate' (derived largely from French), while informal English is largely Anglo-Saxon, the usage, still, of those who had been – and remained? – conquered. Middle- and upper-middle class English now is distinct from working-class and lower-class English, in its words and to some extent in its syntax. This is reflected in a set of different words for the two groups: not only the Anglo-Saxon *cow* for those who tended the *cattle* of the lord, the French *beef* for those who enjoyed it on their meal tables (matched by countless others which still repeat and maintain this class distinction: *calf* vs *veal*, *swine* and *pig* vs *pork*; but also *wood* and *forest*, *hamlet* and *village*, etc.).

Schonell's reading test perpetuates this distinction with astonishing precision, though it adds Greek-derived words to its classification system: at the lower reading levels there Anglo-Saxon words are in overwhelming majority; at the higher levels the words are exclusively latinate/French; at the highest levels they are Greek and latinate/French in origin (Example 2.17).

But all this time other influences were at work. Christianity brought with it, in the sixth century, a new wave of Latin words (the original Roman Latin persisting on the whole only in place names: the -caster, -caister , -cester, -chester of so many places in England perpetuating the Roman *ceastrum*, the fortified military post or town). The scholarly work of the sixteenth and seventeenth centuries – the inkhorn grammarians mentioned before – attempted to bring order, regularity, 'logic' to this wildly prolific and abundant set of language systems. Looking back to the original Latin they put the never pronounced *b* back into *doubt*, *debt*, for instance, to recover the lost Latin origin. Greek similarly enjoyed a new period of growth in English, as a result of the introduction of learned terms both newly imported and newly invented by the philosophers, scientists, medical people,

Schonell Graded Word Reading Test

tree	little	milk	egg	book
school	sit	frog	playing	bun
flower	road	clock	train	light
picture	think	summer	people	something
dream	downstairs	biscuit	shepherd	thirsty
crowd	sandwich	beginning	postage	island
saucer	angel	ceiling	appeared	gnome
canary	attractive	imagine	nephew	gradually
smoulder	applaud	disposal	nourished	diseased
university	orchestra	knowledge	audience	situated
physics	campaign	choir	intercede	fascinate
forfeit	siege	recent	plausible	prophecy
colonel	soloist	systematic	slovenly	classification
genuine	institution	pivot	conscience	heroic
pneumonia	preliminary	antique	susceptible	enigma
oblivion	scintillate	satirical	sabre	beguile
terrestrial	belligerent	adamant	sepulchre	statistics
miscellaneous	procrastinate	tyrannical	evangelical	grotesque
ineradicable	judicature	preferential	homonym	fictitious
rescind	metamorphosis	somnambulist	bibliography	idiosyncrasy

Example 2.17

The Schonell Graded Word Reading Test presents, in a quite remarkably pure form, a particular piece of the history of English, a statement about the English system of social class, and the unrecognized appearance of both in the field of education and literacy.

The first six lines consist, with few exceptions, of words that derive from the Anglo-Saxon, that is, the Germanic, origins of English (the exceptions are flower, playing, train, picture, people, biscuit, postage) i.e. 7 out of 30 words. The next four lines move decisively away from that origin, and towards the period of French influence: only 4 (gnome, angel, smoulder, knowledge) out of 20 words are of Anglo-Saxon origin; the others are of romance-language origin, or, in the case of orchestra, from Greek.

From there downward, Anglo-Saxon has disappeared; words of romance-language origin dominate, whether from French or directly from Latin (as in the case of terrestrial, homonym, somnambulist).

The further down the page one goes the greater also the influence of Greek-derived words, the words of science, medicine, and of certain other professions.

In other words, what looks on the face of it like a simple test of knowledge of words and their spellings, is in fact an uncovering of where, in the social hierarchy of this society, a child (and her/his parents) is located: English, the language and the society, still preserve, in very many ways, the effects of the Norman conquest, which made French the language of the ruling class, and made Anglo-Saxon (in reality a collection of about seven quite distinct Germanic dialects) the language of those who toiled in the fields, in the castles, in the palaces and workshops. What presents itself as the neutral instrument of a test of knowledge, the spelling test, is a test of social origin, location, and affiliation.

mathematicians of that period. When all this is added to the great sound-shift of the late fourteenth century, which had the effect of making Chaucer's language more distant from present-day English than it might otherwise be (for instance, it made the -*gh*- as in *Knight* silent; until then it had been sounded as in German *Knecht*, a sound as in Scottish *loch*), the complexity of present-day English begins to become clearer.

In later chapters I shall focus specifically on much more recent loanwords – from around other parts of Europe and the rest of the world. Here it is sufficient to say that this kind of history alone is sufficient to ensure that 'logic', in its usual everyday sense of a system with a relatively easily deduced regularity, is not what we can expect from English and its spelling. But the situation is worse than this, because to this condensed history of the linguistic origins of modern English we have to add the history of the alphabet itself – in its travels for 5000–6000 years or so from early Egyptian hieroglyphics to Semitic languages such as Phoenician (where it was used to transcribe **syllables**, not single sounds) via early Greece to Rome, and on to the different parts of Europe at various later times. That history is truly one of enormous complexity. The old and standard assumption was that an effective alphabetic system would be one in which for every one sound there would be one letter symbol. But in the journey from one language to the next, an alphabet is constantly used to transcribe the sounds of languages for which it was never designed – and in the process the ideal of the one-sound–one-letter correspondence simply evaporates. The examples are too well known to list: they are examples that show that the long *i* sound as in *key* can also be spelled as in *marine*, or *meet*, or *mete*, or *meat*, or *perceive*, or *belief*, etc.; or that the long *u* sound as in *rude* can be spelled as in *blew*, or *move*, or *true*, or *troop*, or *Jules*, etc.

Superimposed on the two distinct histories of language origin and the writing system is a further significant history: that of scribal practices. The scribes of medieval European courts and administrations had their own practices, and adhered to 'fashions' that had European-wide effects. For instance, the dot on our *i* is a scribal invention, as is the letter *j*, which was used originally simply as a form of *i* in word final position. Our present use of *g* as in *gem*, or *generate*, and the use of *j* for the same sound, as in *juggle*, or *judicial*, is a spelling we owe to the joint effects of Norman French and various scribal practices.

For someone like myself this sort of stuff needs to come with a health warning; I could spend all the hours of a day following up these tiny bits of evidence of vast historical events and movements. I can see, however, that not everyone will find all of this equally consuming; and so my reason for giving this condensed history is not so much to indulge a personal foible, as to point out that English spelling yields up its sense and its order only through the pursuit of histories of this kind, though done in much greater detail. And the point of saying this is that there are fiercely insistent tendencies in certain approaches to the teaching of spelling, which proceed from the assumption that the system of English spelling as such is 'logical', and that it can be made to yield up its logic, if only one persists with the application of some learnable rules. I want to assert by contrast that the system of English spelling consists of a multiplicity of systems of often entirely different origin, entirely different ages and histories, often deeply contradictory, so that there is no **single** logic or principle of coherence that a student of English spelling could follow with any real hopes of success.

I am strongly of the view that to teach spelling on the basis of its inherent logic makes the task impossible for many both of the brightest, and of the least able. The brightest will quickly see the lack of coherence, the absence of logic and system, and will turn their back not only on an incoherent system but also on those who seemingly cannot see that that is the case. The weakest will take it as yet more evidence of their insufficiency, and further confirmation of their inadequacy. They too will turn away.

I want children to learn to spell. I think that the most damaging procedure is to pursue an incoherent route with authoritiarian vigour. I think that the most effective and intellectually beneficial route is to declare, quite simply, that the sense of the system lies both in a history of vast complexity and in a present that is complex for yet further reasons. Parts of this system have to be learned simply by rote because their logics are too difficult to untangle, while other parts can be made to reveal their historical origins and interest quite readily. That would make spelling a worthwhile part of any education.

2.5 Language and spelling

I mentioned at the beginning of this chapter that I would not give a theory of language here. I did want to show, however, some of the kinds of things we need to attend to if we want a more than superficial – and misleading – idea of what spelling is. My assumption is that children probably first spell visually: that is, they **see** language-as-writing, and in copying that, they are **spelling**. That means that we have to attend to the visuality of language. Children start by asking, 'How do you **write** Joanna?', and I assume that they expect as an answer a 'picture' of what they wish to write. It is much later that they begin to ask 'How do you **spell** Joanna?' Children are the most acute and astute analysts of the sounds of language. Their ears are sharp and their hearing is fresh; unlike us they hear what is there rather than what they are meant to hear. What they hear is English (or any language) in the multiplicity of varieties in which it occurs. So we need a sense of language not as an abstract system, but of how it actually is. Spelling depends on a clear sense of what the units of meaning are; it depends on grammar and on meaning as much as it depends on sound and sight. The spelling of English is not 'logical', and given the history of what is now the English language it really couldn't be. And so we need a sense of the history of the language if *we* want to get a sense of the real difficulties involved.

Chapter 3

The many meanings of spelling

3.1 The commonsense, and a different view: spelling as making meaning

It may seem unusual, to say the least, to think of spelling as a system for **making** meaning, rather than as a system for **reproducing** meaning; or, to use an older idiom, for accurately 'rendering meaning'. However, it seems to me that in any serious, closer look at the spellings of young people – really from their very first efforts, from the ages of 2 or 3 years on up to, say, the ages of 8, 9 or 10 – what we see is the attempt to make meaning with, and out of, this system. (This is not to ignore adults' attempts in the same direction, as my example of the *cyclemen* in Chapter 1 is meant to show.)

I would like to make a distinction here that seems especially important in relation to spelling: the distinction between **making meaning with** a system, as against **making sense of** that system. **Making sense of** is what I think we usually have in mind when we think of children learning to spell: 'Here is a system; yes, admittedly, it is not entirely straightforward; but with effort you'll be able to make sense of it'. **Making sense of** learning a system is a clear step up from learning a system by rote, learning without understanding. By contrast it seems to me that young spellers, left to their own devices, treat spelling as a means with which to make meaning. This is not to say that they don't experiment, that they don't puzzle; or that their efforts do not show constant analysis, re-analysis, restart and remaking of assumptions. It is to say that for children spelling is an active system for the making of their meaning.

So let me make this point once more, as clearly as I can. Children make their meanings with anything that is to hand: with spoken language of course, but equally with things around the house – with chairs, pillows, blankets, boxes; with pens and paint and paper; with Lego bricks or wooden blocks; and so on. We all assume that they make meaning when they first learn to speak, and then when they learn to write. All of us take it absolutely for granted that that is what the learning of language is about. Most of us think that that is what children's play is about. It is simply inconceivable to me that they would suspend that absolute disposition towards making meaning that characterizes their actions towards all of their world when it comes to this one tiny aspect of it, to spelling. The problem for children is the adults' commonsense, which insists that spelling is a routinized convention that is devoid of meaning. The adults' insistence on the meaninglessness of spelling becomes a huge problem for child speakers because it expresses the adults' concerns with 'getting it correct' in terms of convention, while children's concern is with 'getting it right' in terms of meaning. 'Getting it correct' derives from attitudes to power and authority, whereas 'getting it right' derives from attitudes to truthfulness and knowledge.

To see 'invented spelling' in this way is by no means new. Many others before me – researchers, scholars, teachers, parents – have recognized this. In this chapter I should like to outline some means by which we can begin to recognize what young spellers are doing. A first step in this attempt is to try to understand what spelling actually is; and that is in part what this book is about. A second step is to try to understand that the phenomenon we call 'spelling' actually consists of many different things all lumped together; it isn't at all one single thing, phenomenon or process. 'Spelling' is a complex of processes and relations, all of them meaningful, but all in different ways. Spelling is a system of resources for making meaning.

I want to introduce one technical term here, and call these resources **semiotic resources**, to indicate that they belong to that vast set of resources – linguistic, visual, three-dimensional, actional, gestural – through which all of us always make our meanings. Children use the various semiotic resources involved in spelling as a means for making their meanings. In this chapter I develop a sketch of a theory in which such an approach is treated as entirely usual. Spelling, like punctuation, is a system that is productive of meaning. Both are, however, subject to very close regulation – spelling more so than punctuation – and so the meaning-making potentials of either of these systems are not readily visible. Both spelling and punctuation seem as though they are 'just how we do things'. In this way spelling seems more like the Highway Code, where we tend not to ask 'Will I drive on the left or on the right side of the road today?', and the idea of 'inventive driving' is very close to 'criminal behaviour'. The rules of spelling seem to be no more than means of enforcing and observing conventions – a bit like eating your peas balanced on the rounded back of your fork. The regulation of these systems is enforced more or less strictly in different places and at different times. I have certainly been in places where driving on the right or on the left is not a matter of either/or, of yes or no, but a matter of more or less, sort of. As I have mentioned earlier, in the later 1960s and 1970s the regulation of spelling was relatively weakly enforced; now in the mid to late1990s the enforcement is much closer.

The meanings that young spellers make in their spellings vary with their shifting interest, and with shifts in their growing awareness and understanding of the potentials of the system. Consequently there are changes that take place over longer stretches of time, and there are changes that happen from moment to moment, owing to changes in the interests of the speller. In Chapters 4 and 5 I show these differing interests, and their developing directions, in greater detail. At this point I wish to make some comments that restate in part what I have said in Chapters 1 and 2, and then build on that to outline a specific approach to an understanding of children's spelling.

So, to recapitulate and to remind ourselves: the commonsense view, by and large, is that to spell is to transliterate, to transcribe sound into graphic form, to turn sounds into letters. This assumes a rough and ready equivalence between the elements of the sound system of a language – its vowels, sounds such as *a*, *i*, *u*, which are made without obstruction to the air as it leaves the mouth, and with the vocal chords vibrating to produce 'voice'; its semi-vowels, sounds such as the *j* in yacht, or the *w* in water, made with slight obstruction; consonants, in which the passage of the air is obstructed in a significant way; diphthongs and triph-thongs, in which either two or three vowels are run together, *ai* as in time, or *aia* as in fire – with individual letters or with stable combinations of letters (*gh*, *ch*, *ou*, *ie*, etc.) if need be. Here is how this was put in a nineteenth-century grammar book 2.

(J.M.D. Meiklejohn, *The English Language. Its Grammar, History, and Literature*, London: Alfred M. Holden 1899, p. 7):

> An alphabet is, as we have seen, a code of signs or signals. Every code of signs has two laws, neither of which can be broken without destroying the accuracy and trustworthiness of the code. These two laws are:
>
> i.   One and the same sound must be represented by one and the same let-ter. (Hence: No sound should be represented by more than one letter.)
> ii. One letter or set of letters must represent only one and the same sound. (Hence: No letter should represent more than one sound.)
>
> Or, put in another way:
>
> i.   One sound must be represented by one distinct symbol.
> ii. One symbol must be translated to the ear by no more than one sound.
>
> i.   The first is broken when we represent the long sound of *a* in eight dif-ferent ways, as in – fate, braid, say, great, neigh, prey, gaol, gauge.
> ii. The second is broken when we give eight different sounds to the one sym-bol *ough*, as in – bough, cough, dough, hiccough (= cup), hough = hock), tough, through, thorough.

I have quoted from a staid old source lest critics accuse me of being trivially fash-ionable; but also to indicate that these facts have been well recognized over a very long time.

We know that this ideal is never met in any language, and it certainly is not in English. In Chapter 2 I have indicated some reasons why it cannot ever be met. This commonsense, just to say it again, makes speech into the origin of writing: speech is what has to be transcribed, 'turning sounds into the visible marks of letters'; and speech has to be fixed, making the non-permanent speech into the permanent written record, in writing, by the means of spelling. Speech is the starting point; and writing is speech 'fixed' and made visible.

Against this commonsense let me put a number of points, some that I have already mentioned and some newly made. In order to spell, you already need to know what the **words** of a language – the larger units of meaning and sound – are. Words exist most obviously and clearly in written form; and that alone ensures that a prior knowledge of the **written** language is essential if you want to spell. In fact we can say that it is the letter shape of words as the units of writing that underlies the rules of spelling. In other words, and to put it bluntly, you could not learn to spell if all you knew was how to **speak** English, and you had a list of the 'rules' for turning sounds into letters. Given that there is no clear correspondence between sounds and letters, when there is a problem the matter is always settled in favour of the already written and **visible** form: '**Look, this** is how it is spelled', pointing to the 'look' of the written form. It is never settled by saying: '**Listen**, this is how it **sounds**, and that's why you spell it like this'; never 'You say *r e s e e t* and **that's** why it is spelled *receipt*'. In order to learn to spell it helps a lot if you can spell already. In order to spell it helps a huge lot more to know **writing** than to know **sounding**. Spelling is founded on the givens of the written language. But to put it like this destroys the commonsense idea of spelling as the 'writing down of speech', of transliterating spoken language into a permanent written form.

Let me consider once more an example I have discussed earlier (Example 3.1).

To spell you need to know the words of the language, both as **sense** units – that is, as units of meaning – and as **sound** units. You need to know that the sound sequence *u a i t s c h o o s* can be either *white shoes* or *why choose*. If you hear the sound sequence *uaitschoos* the simple rules – such as they are – of transliterating sounds into letters, won't tell you which it is. Early medieval writing was in fact much closer to a simple transliteration of sounds into letters in that word boundaries were not indicated. Letters were written in a continuous sequence, without the gaps that now indicate the boundaries of words for us: itwaswrittenlikethis. Many of the gaps that exist between words in writing are not there in speech; they are produced by the writing system.

In that respect, spelling acts as a framing and as a punctuation of what is for the most part a continuous stream of sound in speech. As the *white shoes/why choose* example shows, the boundaries between words-as-sound-units or words-as-meaning that units need not be present or marked in speech. This is not to say that speakers of a language which has no writing aren't fully aware of words-as-sense-units, or of words-as-sound-units. They know the words *white, shoes, why, choose*, and yet might not hear a clear gap between these when they are spoken normally. Spelling is a punctuation of the stream of sound into 'chunks' of meaning and of sound, when it transliterates sound into graphic form. For literate speakers, the image of the written form acts as a visual memory, which is silently carried as a frame for the 'chunking' of sound even in speaking, even when that speech is not transcribed.

Example 3.1

Spelling is based on writing

Here are (the) two (first) definitions of spelling, one from the *Concise Oxford Dictionary* and the other from the (Australian) *Macquarie Dictionary*.
From the *Concise Oxford Dictionary:*

write or name (in correct sequence) the letters that form (a word,...)

and from the *Macquarie Dictionary*:

to name, write, or otherwise give (as by signals) in order, the letters of (a word, a syllable, etc.)

The reference to 'letters' in both definitions makes it clear that what is at issue is writing. So neither dictionary puts forward what I have called the commonsense view: that is, that spelling is the process of transliterating the sounds of speech into the letters of writing. However, that isn't a great help for the child who has only heard the word, or for a learner of English as a second or other language who is in the same position.

To be able to spell, by the definitions of both dictionaries, is a simple matter: you have to be able to spell; you need to know the letters in their correct sequence. This puts **writing** first. But children (as most learners of a language) meet language in spoken form. This speller knows the word *sharpener*; as a word she has heard, probably many times. But that, as I pointed out in Example 1.1, is in no way sufficient to **spell** the word.

However, as I suggested in Chapter 2, writing probably starts for most or all children in our present period, and in developed societies, **not** as the transcription of sound into letters but as the **drawing** of a particular bit of the visual environment. We have all heard of or experienced the 2-year-old in the car or pushchair who recognizes the letters or the letter-logo of shops or fast-food outlets. The early attempts by children at the writing of their names, just as much as the usually somewhat later 'drawings of writing' – whether as letters and sequences of letters or as what seems to be the drawing of lines of print – are visual representations of parts of the visual environment. Examples 3.2 and 3.3 show evidence of this.

In my own experience (limited to the observation of our children and of their friends) children tend, in their early writing, to focus on the activity of **writing** and not on the activity of **spelling**. Typically they will say: 'How do you **write** Charley?' rather than 'How do you **spell** Charley?'. What they seem to expect as a response to their request at that stage is a visual model of the written form that they can use as a model for what is in fact the **drawing** of the name, rather than a spoken **spelling** to reproduce by transliteration into graphic form. They expect a written model produced on a page, rather than a sounding out of letter names. It is quite likely, although this is subject to great debate, that writing itself, as a human cultural achievement, started as drawing or as some other graphic/visual representation, quite independently of the spoken language, and not as a recording or transliteration of sound. Much later in human history this separately developed system of drawing as representation became subordinated to spoken language as a means of its recording, of its fixing, as its visual transliteration in some cultures, though by no means in all. In pictographic and ideographic writing such as Chinese, for instance, this subordination of visual representation to sound did not happen. Such a history of writing accords with my own small-scale observation of the path children take into their manner of the representation of their world. It can take a route as the recording of that world through the drawing of some object, or it can take a route that is the expression of meanings, a wish to express aspects of the 'inner world' of the drawer. Example 3.4 shows early drawing, and 3.5 an instance of what may be more like 'expression'.

These two paths – the one **recording** the outer world (representation) and the other **expressing** the inner world (expression) – are, of course, always intertwined in some way. Nothing can be recorded outwardly that hasn't first been transformed in the 'inner world', to use that way of speaking. The expressive aspects of children's sign-making have a development that leads into the ever greater articulation of their representational capabilities: either by becoming subsumed into the mode of writing and of its development; or by being drawn into the modes of drawing, of painting, of modelling and so on. Just to show what I mean I will reproduce here an example (3.6) that I have used before – the move from **circular scribbles** to **circles** to **circles as a means of representation**. I think that this example shows the path from **expression of feelings** to deliberate, articulate, 'rational' **representation of ideas**.

Spelling, in the non-commonsensical sense of **representing and 'fixing' elements of the (external) world**, including representing language in visual form, starts long before *sounding*. The question arises: what unites these very different aspects of 'spelling'? In my view it is that they are all instances, in some way or other, of **translation**. As with any translation, the original is always so complex that a translation can only ever represent some aspects of the original, namely those that the translator feels are most important in what is to be translated.

Here I shall put forward three principles that I believe are always at issue in the activity of translation that we call **spelling**. First: the shift from sounds to letters is a shift in the **mode of representation**, from the physical substance of sound into the graphic substance of writing. So the first unifying principle is that in spelling we record things that exist in one kind of substance, one mode of representation, in a different kind of substance, a different mode of representation.

> Spelling is a translation from one material medium – in this case sound – into another material medium, graphic substance.

Braille is another instance of a translation from one representational mode to another: from **sound** organized as speech to **touch** organized as three-dimensional configurations of marks on an otherwise flat surface. I call this move from one material medium to another **transduction**.

The second principle is that spelling is **transformation**. The shift from sound to visual images, for instance, always brings with it inevitable and substantive changes, owing to the differing potentials of the modes. You can do things with sound that you cannot do with graphic substance, and vice versa. Certain things can be done easily in one mode and not at all easily in another mode. The temporal/sequential nature of speech sounds enables certain things to be done that are less or not at all possible in the spatial/simultaneous mode of graphic representation; and the possibilities of tactile apprehension, as in the reading of the Braille script, differ yet again both from the perception of sound by the ear and from the perception of graphic substance by the eye. In other words, it matters, in quite fundamental ways, in what mode the 'spelling' happens: it affects what can be spelled; and it affects how it can be 'taken up', perceived by its readers/viewers/sensors.

The mode in which spelling happens also affects what information and what kind of information is available to the 'reader'. As a person who has both sight and hearing I can only attempt to imagine in the most superficial ways what kinds of information I take absolutely for granted in visually reading a page; or in being a hearing person in the environment of sound. I imagine that the precision of (and preciseness about) information required for the sense of touch in the 'reading' of Braille script will make the reader of that script 'take up' information in quite particular ways, and think in entirely different ways about what reading is, and what abilities and dispositions it is founded on, than I do with my ability to see and hear.

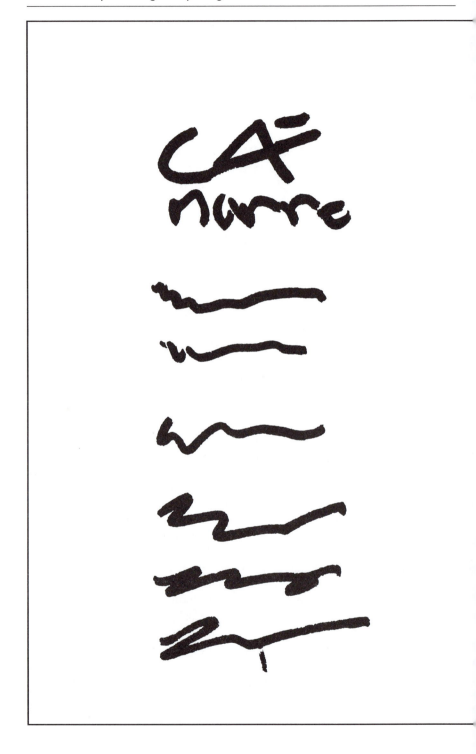

Example 3.2

Spelling as the drawing of a part of the visual environment

The visual environment of contemporary 'developed' societies (especially capitalist consumerist societies with their heavy use of advertising) is saturated with writing, in all possible forms. All of us, children included, can only ever attend to a small part of that environment. That attention is in part an effect of the environment – bright lights, bold colours, striking images – and in part an effect of our selective looking, which is guided by our interest.

Children see more than adults – they have not yet developed the filters that edit out the things that we don't want to see. But children's seeing is also guided by their interest; because their interest often differs from ours so deeply, they astonish us by what they see.

Here the child's interest had been prompted by a first visit to a bank in France, with her family; and the experience of all the paraphernalia of setting up an account led her and her brother to a long period of playing 'banks'.

The two or three general points that emerge are: the visual environment is saturated with print; a child's interest in parts of that environment is engaged selectively, as is that of adults; and children are likely to meet the alphabet and writing long before they meet 'spelling' in the sense of the translation of sound to letter.

In this example the child has drawn the letter-logo, focusing clearly on the shape of the letters. Because her interest was in setting up her own 'branch' of this bank, she has also written out the name of the branch. Below, she has drawn some lines of print. Here she has not focused on individual letter shapes, but rather on the 'look', as if from a distance, of the lines of print. Here her interest in what she wants to represent is clearly different: here she is focused on 'the look of the print' rather than the shape of letters. She wants to indicate 'there is writing here', but isn't bothered to show what this writing is in detail.

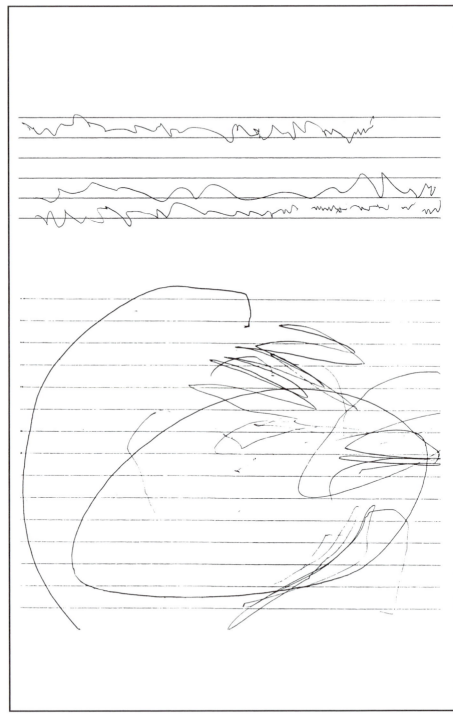

Example 3.3

Drawing writing: the shifting focus on print

To someone who is fully familiar with alphabetic writing, the complexities of the system are no longer apparent, and the constant shifts in focus that we engage in, in relation to writing and the environment of print, have sunk below our threshold of awareness. In children's early engagement with print these shifts in focus are clearly visible. They reveal the many different facets of the world of the print environment, and they reveal the shifting focus and interest of children in relation to print.

In the 'lines of print' example, the child has obviously focused on the appearance of print in long and connected lines. No doubt she has also seen her parents writing such lines, and she produces, for herself, that aspect of writing. Just four months earlier (at the age of 2 years and 9 months) her writing looked very different. Not focused on lines; not focused on the connection between elements; indeed, 'elements' are hardly the issue.

In neither of these two cases is there any question of a transcription/translation/transduction from sound to letter: writing is visual; writing is spatial; writing is drawing; writing is the making of an image.

(Continued on pages 92–93)

Example 3.3 (continued)

That is still the case some two years later, when the child seems to be practising letter shapes, though she called it 'doing my writing' (at 4 years and 11 months). At this age a clear shift has happened, as seen in the last example on the opposite page. This example is a newspaper page; it is the news, which was 'They were having a conference in America. There was a burglar who broke into somebody's window'. It is not clear to me whether this is, for the child, a transcription of speech as 'sound and meaning', or a transcription of the meaning alone. If it is a transcription of 'sound and meaning' then it shows the child's sense of spelling moving towards the idea of a transduction from sound to letters. Of course it still remains graphic; it is still a drawing.

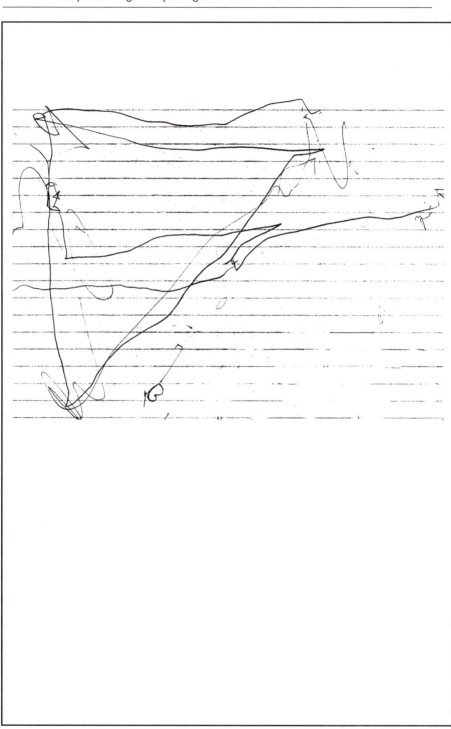

Example 3.4

Early drawing: the representation of meaning

This drawing was made by a child at the age of 2 years and 1 month. One context for it is the child's avid watching on TV of a cartoon adventure narrative of a young child, Sebastian, and his St Bernard dog, Belle.

Child: I want to draw
Father: OK then, but just one picture, 'cause I've got to go.
As he was drawing he said:
Child: I'm going to draw a lake, a stream, for Belle and Bastian, and a
       rock too,
       and a mountain too.
       Look there's a bear, wrroww.

I take this to be 'representational' in the sense of recording a recollection of an episode of the adventure. The lines and shapes of the drawing are outwardly made traces of this recollection. The shapes and lines represent the lake, the stream, the mountain (the adventure is set in the high Pyrenees). They were made as an accompaniment – a recording? – of the events and the objects encountered.

Example 3.5

The expression of meaning

This drawing was made nine months earlier than the drawing of Example 3.4. It is quite typical of the graphic expression of children at that age (and for the following two years or so): it has stabbing, jabbing movements; it also has the straight lines produced by the child's back and forth movements of her or his hand, some circular movements, and some lines drawn as 'free-standing' elements, 'just lines'.

I feel that these different movements, and their graphic traces, point to quite distinct affective and cognitive attitudes: the stabbing/jabbing move is, in my view, much more an 'action on' the environment – the page – a transitive action, than the lines drawn as free-standing lines, which seem more like 'making a mark'.

The important points for me are these: quite different feelings and/or attitudes give rise to, and are expressed by, the different features; this drawing seems more **expressive** of inner states than the representation of Example 3.4; these aspects of drawing remain with, and adhere to drawing, even when drawing becomes the highly regulated representation of the conventionalized shapes of letters. This means that affect remains with and effects the production of letters – alphabetic writing is not stripped of emotion and affect, it is never purely 'rational'.

Of course, it is this that gives rise to the practice of 'reading' handwriting for traces of the writer's personality.

Example 3.6

From expression to representation

These four drawings (repeated once more for my purposes here) illustrate one path that children travel on the road from expression to what the adult world might regard as 'rational' representation. I said in my comment on Example 3.5 that in my view all representation has aspects of affect. In other words, when we communicate about something, our emotions and feelings are always involved as well; and all expression is representational, which means that, when we seem to be simply showing feeling and emotion, we always communicate something else at the same time. Nevertheless, alphabetic – and no doubt other – cultures do make a distinction between the two, more or less firmly, more or less enforced.

The first drawing seems to me to be the effect of the child's exuberance and energy: he is expressing himself through circularity rather than linearity, through roundness and smoothness rather than through jaggedness and sharpness; and these are clearly the affective meanings. Over a period of some two years, roundness, smoothness and circularity, is developed by the child into the abstractness of 'circle'. I would want to insist that in this child's circles, made at the age of 3, there is still the trace of energy, enthusiasm, roundness – but now generalized to the abstract notion of 'circle'.

It is roundness as 'going round and round' that lends itself so easily to making circles metaphors for wheels, and wheels can then equally easily become a metaphor for car – where 'car-ness' is, for this child, at this age, most aptly represented by 'wheelness', with all the energy and movement of 'going round and round'.

For me there is another crucial point: adult society, of course, already has the concept of 'circle'. Nevertheless, this child has made this concept for himself; he has made this abstract, rational concept out of the expression of affective states. I see no reason why this should be at all different in the child's move into lettered representation; no reason why feeling, emotion, affect should be lost in the drawing of letter shapes when the child learns to write.

Spelling usually, perhaps always, involves shifting across modes, the action that I have called transduction – 'moving across' – and that has transformative effects (Examples 3.7, 3.8).

But a shift **within one mode**, as in a child's representation of writing in her or his drawing, is also transformative. The examples that I have given so far, whether of the 'thank you' in (Example 2.11), or the examples in this chapter, illustrate this. Example 3.9 is one more example to make this point.

Spelling inevitably changes that which is spelled, and these changes are due not to whim or accident but to the interest of the speller and the potentials of the mode in which the spelling happens. 'Spelling' a spoken utterance is to take out the tone of the voice, emotion, effect and personal characteristics of the speaker such as gender, age, social and regional background, and so on. Spelling is, inevitably, transformative and therefore creative. This flies in the face of the commonsense that spelling is par excellence an area where rote learning, either of 'rules' or of individual items (my example of *commitment*, or is it *committment?*) rather than creative production holds sway. I shall come to this in a moment, in discussing the general issue of copying. In children's spelling this creativity is still plain to see; it is harder to notice it with those who have fully entered into the conventions of their social group.

The third principle that unites all forms of spelling is that of **recording**. Recording has two relatively distinct aspects. As the word indicates, it provides or makes a record, an object, an objectified version of some element or event in the world. It also acts as and provides a **fixing**, either as in the chemical 'fixing' of the emulsion of the photograph, or the fixing of an event as in the countless snapshot photographs of humans: 'fixing' a young person in a moment of childhood; or 'fixing' the moment of a significant event – the christening, the birthday party, the momentary pose or the quick glance.

For the purposes of my rudimentary theory here I shall say that spelling is always an action that has three aspects: that of translation, which I shall call **transduction** from one mode to another; that of **transformation**, in one or more of many different possible ways; and that of **recording**. These three principles operate in all spelling, in different mixes, and with different emphases on one or other of the three. Even in the case that seems weakest, that of a child's drawing of writing, the original 'stuff' of print is different from the 'stuff' of the hand-drawn version in the child's drawn spelling: so that to the child at least it may seem as a shift across modes, as a kind of translation/transduction. Of course, as I hope to show (Examples 3.10–3.12 are given on pp. 108–15 and 118–19) there is no question whether transformation and recording are present. They are clearly there: the drawn writing is a transformation of the original, and, clearly, it records and fixes the child's understanding of writing at this point.

The fact that there are always (at least) three aspects involved enables us to make better sense of the many and varied difficulties that can arise for children in spelling. For some children the shift across modes seems a big problem: this is an issue I raise in a later chapter. For instance, the translation/transduction from the temporal sequence of sound in speech to the spatial linearity of the sequence of letters in writing may be one of the fundamental difficulties in that broad range of problems collected under the label **dyslexia**.

3.2 'Copying'

Given that transduction, transformation and recording are always involved in spelling, 'copying' is unlikely to be an appropriate way of thinking about spelling. And yet 'copying' is, I think, the underpinning commonsense assumption of most approaches to spelling. This is so whether it is copying in the guise of rote learning – 'just copy what you see' or more usually 'just copy what you hear' – or whether the issue is the learning of rules (by rote) that will enable you to produce perfect copies each time you apply them. As far as **transformation** goes, the possible routes that transformation can take are very large in number; perhaps they are infinitely many. What gets transformed, and how, depends on the decisions of the speller. Those decisions arise out of the speller's interest, now, at this moment of spelling. On pp. 112–13 I give a first example, 3.11, of how I think we need to look at this.

The principles that I draw from this are these.

1   First and foremost, copying may be a consciously held intention, but it is never a reality.
2   The 'copy' exhibits the principles or criteria of relevance that the 'copier' applied in making the 'copy'.
3   A 'copy' is always a new making, and the new making is the result of two factors. On the one hand, it is a factor of aspects of the things copied; and on the other hand, it is a factor of the criteria applied by the copier. What looks like mere 'copying' is always new making.
4   Because of principles 2 and 3 we can attempt to deduce what the 'interest' of the maker of the 'copy' was, at the point when she or he made it. We can speculate on reasonable grounds about what was in the copier's thoughts when she or he made the copy.

This sequence allows us to treat 'invented spellings' genuinely as **inventions**, as something newly made in the context of a particular set of circumstances, always drawing on what was available to make this new thing with. 'Invention' is therefore never invention in its more negative sense of 'just made up', 'just dreamed up' – which is one popular meaning of 'invented spelling' – or of meanings implicit in '(just) pure invention' – that is, as having no relation to reality. Children's invented spellings are very much related to reality – to two realities in fact: to the reality of the world that is the prompt for their spelling, and to the reality of the world of their own interests, which guides how they make sense of the world and which guides their spelling.

Let me briefly explore the implications in practice of these four principles: (1)

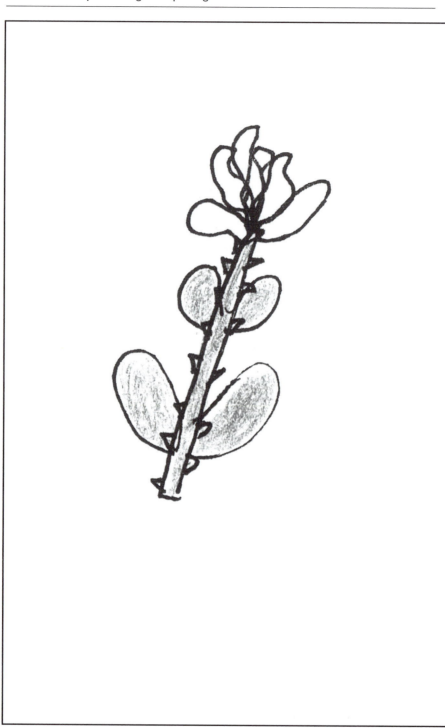

Example 3.7

Spelling as transduction: moving from one kind of substance to another

Bringing the natural, physical world into the domain of culture involves many processes, among which two are perhaps central: first, the physical world has to be 'captured' in a different medium, a medium of representation – whether it is sound that is 'captured' electronically as in sound recording, or light that is 'captured' chemically as in photography, or the sounds of speech that are 'captured' graphically as letters. Not all the aspects of the physical world are or can be represented: only those that can be 'captured' in that medium, and only those that both the culture and the individual who does the representing wish to be represented.

In this drawing of an actual rose, growing in the family's garden, the three-dimensionality of the natural world has become two-dimensional; there is no possibility of touching, of smelling or of seeing the rose at different times in different light. The child's imagination was clearly engaged by the brightness of the yellow (in the original), and by the thorns, which are, on the rose in the garden, exceptionally large, tightly spaced and sharp. These are the features that the child has selected, and which she has made particularly prominent. All spelling involves a shift in the medium of representation; all spelling selects and brings certain characteristics into prominence. In this way all spelling is transformative.

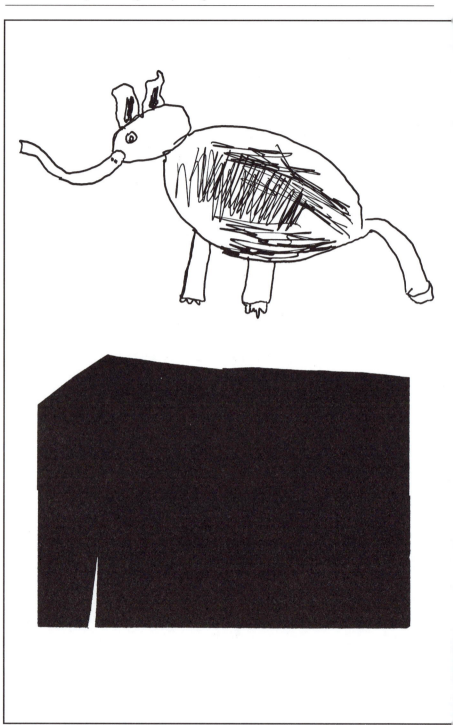

Example 3.8

Spelling and the potentials of the materials used for spelling

With the previous example, 3.7, I attempted to show that not every facet and characteristic of 'the thing to be spelled' either is or can be spelled. With the two examples here I want to focus specifically on the fact that the medium that we use for representing something makes a difference: it can make it difficult or even impossible to represent certain characteristics of the thing that is to be represented; or it can lend itself particularly well to representing certain aspects of the thing to be represented, and can make it more likely that specific characteristics are represented; or it can demand particular skills in the use of the medium from the person who does the representing.

The two elephants here were made by the same child, at age 6; she and her friends were sitting around a table drawing elephants; and, using coloured tissue-paper, cutting out the shapes of elephants. One point of interest for me was to see the very different ideas of elephants that the children produced; but that is not the focus here. In the contrast between these two elephants, both represented side-on, in profile so to speak, one child's notion of 'elephantness' is influenced by what she has to hand for making the representation: pens and paper in one case, and scissors and coloured tissue-paper in the other. One set of means leads to the representation of what she regards as criterial features: the trunk, the big ears, the tail, the big body. The other set of means leads to the representation of criterial features that do, of course, resemble those of the drawn elephant – the shape of the elephant in outline, the suggested trunk and head – but focus much more insistently on the bulkiness of the animal, on volume and shape, rather than on detail.

In thinking about spelling, even in the conventional sense, this is an important question: What can actually be spelled (and what can **not** be spelled) with the means available, in the case of writing, with the letters of the alphabet?

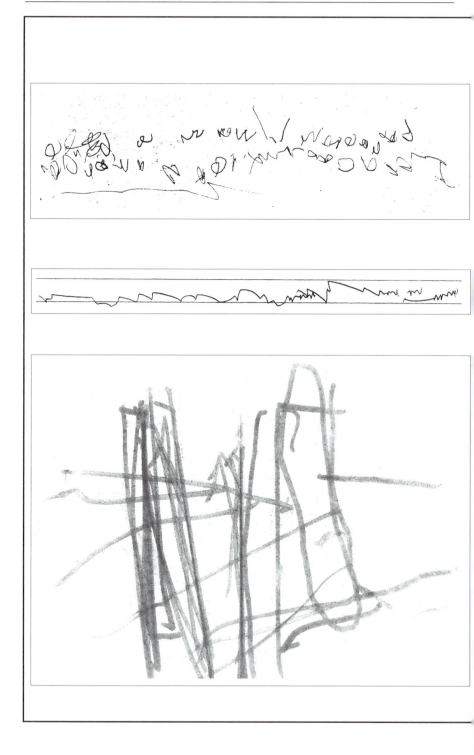

Example 3.9

Spelling as writing: spelling as transformative action

In the two lines of writing here (done at age 3 years and 10 months) the child seems to have focused on several characteristics: the roundness of letters, the connectedness of letters: in other words, this may be 'cursive writing', 'joined-up writing' as teachers and children in primary school call it.

In the other example here, a 'letter' (to a friend, done about nine months earlier), writing appears in a totally different way. Now it is not letters and their connection that are the focus, but the lines of the genre of the letter, its layout, the letter (and writing) as a visual block of text.

As in the example given before, it is the child's shifting focus, itself a reflection of the child's shifting interest, that makes her or him look at different aspects of writing as print, and represent them in this transformed fashion.

will be rocing + a rouing till the
comeing on the mornig will_ _ _ _ _ _
_ _ _ _ _ brack of day.will be _ _ _ _
+ a rouing _   _   _   ⌒

⌒ shake Radel + Role X 4

4oth time shake Radel + Role
ow babby Shake it to me.
Shogen doger wop bam bom x4
                          babby
4ot time Shogen doger wop bam
bom ⚙ Shogen doger wop bam
boloner

Example 3.10

Transduction: moving from one means of representation to another

The two examples here are two more instances of moving from one means of representation to another. I have called it **transduction** to distinguish it from translation, which we usually think of as a process in which meaning is moved within the same means of representation. In translating *War and Peace* we stay within language as our means of representation; though of course we understand that Russian differs from English in important ways. In transduction we do not stay within the same means of representation; this complicates the process enormously.

The first example (on the facing page) results from the performance of a 'show' by several children; and for this they needed a script, both for the 'show' and for songs and other items in it. So it is a case where music and words had to be transcribed, drawn across into a different medium of representation. None of the children knew musical notation, so they had to invent a notational system, which in this case consists of letters and words and dashes as graphic marks. Because the children all knew the songs in question the transcriptional system served well enough.

The children's solution, for instance, of transcribing *shogen doger wop bam bom* is a nice illustration of a problem for spelling: it does not work unless a written version already exists. What is the official (dictionary) written spelling of *shogen doger wop bam bom*?

(Continued on pages 110–111)

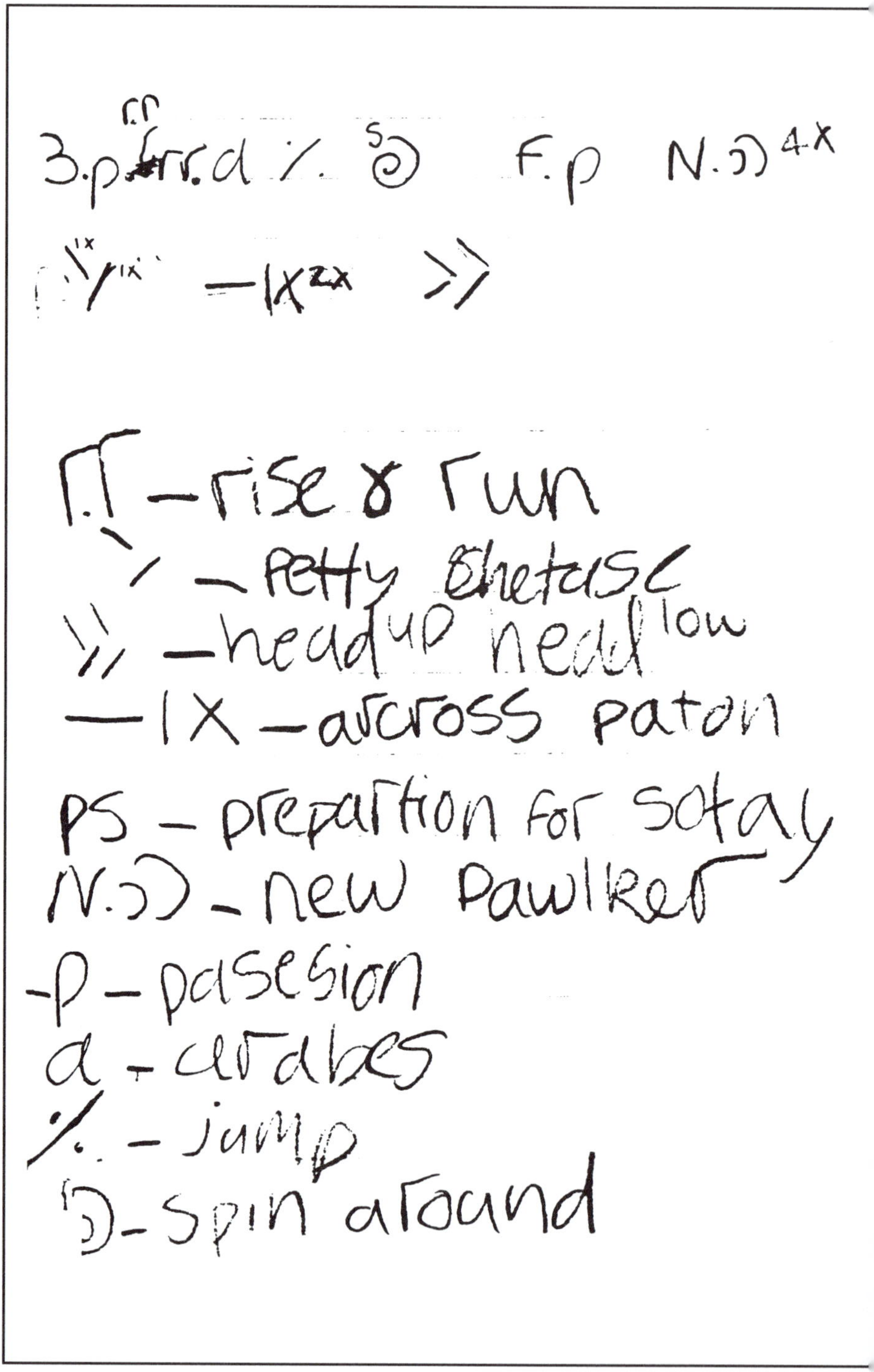

$$3.p \, \overline{\Gamma\Gamma.}a \, / . \, \overset{s}{\circledcirc} \quad F.p \quad N.\mathfrak{I})^{4.x}$$

$$\overset{.x}{/}^{ix} \quad -|x^{2x} \quad \gg$$

$\Gamma.\mathcal{J}$ — rise & run

$/$ — petty chetase

$\gg$ — head^{up} ned^{low}

$-|x$ — arcross paton

PS — prepartion for sotay

N.$\mathfrak{I}$ — new pawlker

-P- pasesion

a - arabes

$\%.$ — jump

$\mathfrak{I}$ — spin around

Example 3.10 (continued)

The second example, on the facing page, also comes out of the context of 'doing a show' in this case what had to be transcribed were the steps of a brief balletic sequence.

The child transcriber is aware that the representational system and its elements are not 'transparent' – in the way the rock-n-roll transcription could be thought to be – and so she provides a key to the notational sytem. This shows directly that this child has (at the age of 7 years) a quite abstract grasp of the question of a notational system and its relation to the elements ('steps' and 'positions') and structures to which it refers.

Transformation

These examples, as well as many of my earlier ones, can serve to illustrate the process of transformation. The *shogen doger wop bam bom* is not, in any sense, the same as the cliché of 1950s rock-n-roll (which I might have transcribed as *shoogen doo-ga wop bam boo*); in part its transformation is due to the fact that these young performers hear the 1950s 'covers'. As I suggested, the drawing of the rose is a transformation; among other things, this transformation is due to the fact that the child had pricked her finger on this rose, a fact more likely to make her accentuate the thorns.

Recording

As with transformation, so with recording: the rock-n-roll transcription is an attempt to fix this tune, so that it can be re-performed. And the ballet – sequence is, of course, quite directly a recording.

Example 3.11

'Copying' the sounds of speech

Assume for a moment that spelling is the copying of the sound of a word, or of a sequence of sounds, by means of letters. On pages 112 and 114 is the eight pages of a book made by a (just) 6-year old, *7 Days of Christmas*.

The first page has the word *Satyr* (Santa). I confess that despite the picture I puzzled about what the child had done here. Yet it is likely that this is an accurate transcription: for many speakers the *n* is actually not pronounced. 2, *Saemoks* (same socks/some socks?), seems to have an *s* missing, which may be a mistake. In 3 (stars), the writing direction is reversed; this may be an effect of how the pages of the book unfolded in sequence. I would treat *staes* as an accurate transcription: the vowel sound *e* is used (instead of the *r*, which in most dialects is not pronounced) to indicate a lengthening of the *a*. In 4 (Christmas trees), there is again an accurate transcription: in many people's pronunciation *Christmas* often becomes *smas*, with the initial *chri* and the *t* barely audible, or completely 'swallowed'.

Clearly these are not copies of the written form of these words. Are they copies of the spoken version? I have treated them as accurate transcriptions, but they tend in the direction of focusing on the consonantal sounds; the stronger consonant sounds seem to provide the auditory frame for the child.

(Continued on pages 112–113)

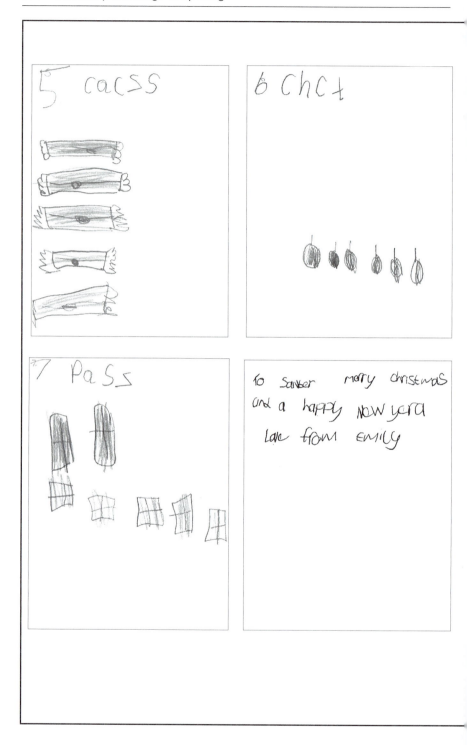

Example 3.11 (continued)

In 5, 6 and 7 this impression is even stronger. In 5, *cacss* (crackers), the spelling seems to mimic the sound of crackers going off; the focus on the consonant sounds *k* and *s* picks out and highlights the explosive quality of the word *crackers*. The doubling of the final *s* may have been the child's means of indicating the plural, but in any case it adds to the strong consonantal sound shape. In both 6 (chocolates) and 7 (parcels), consonants dominate: if the child had put the plural *s* at the end of *chat* this too could be regarded as an accurate transcription. Try saying 'chocolates' minimizing the vowel sounds, and you end up with a sound sequence very close to *chcts*; and similarly with *pass*.

These spellings are evidence of highly acute listening. Are they 'copies'? They all tend in the direction of emphazing consonants over vowels (like the spelling systems of languages such as Arabic or Hebrew). I think this was the principle that the young speller brought to these transcriptions/spellings. They are accurate transcriptions, and yet they are not 'copies' in the usual sense of that word. They are the effects of a systematic transformation, which highlights the auditorily stronger consonantal sounds of words at the expense of the auditorily weaker vowels.

that there is no copying; (2) that the 'copy' exhibits the criteria applied by the maker; (3) that the 'copy' is always new as a joint effect of characteristics of the thing copied and of the criteria applied by the copier; and (4) that the 'copy' therefore gives us insight into the actions and thoughts of the 'copier'.

The first principle forces us away from notions of error or mistake; the new form (the 'copy') exhibits the principles or criteria that the speller applied. This does not force us to give up notions of 'correctness': an incorrect spelling is one in which the criteria applied by the speller did not match the features of the 'correct' spelling that convention insists on. We can therefore have it as a legitimate aim, as I do, to enable all children to spell correctly, without treating their early spellings as error and mistake. Giving up **error** and **mistake** as our first 'port of call' for an explanation of unconventional spelling is essential to get a real understanding of what children are doing in their spelling, their thinking, their take on the world. In order to understand their real abilities, we need to look to the other principles. At the end of that, we could then think freshly about strategies for the teaching and for the learning of 'correct' spelling.

The second principle directs our attention towards the criteria applied by the speller. In the 'Look I've done it' example on pp. 60, I suggested that the child had applied two principles. One was 'Things that are joined up, which are linked, belong together: they are part of the same larger thing'. In this instance the 'thing' was a visual entity, a bit of writing; and the joined-up bits were the lines forming the letters written by the parent. The other principle, perhaps more implicit though equally potent, was 'My father doesn't do things without reason'. A generalized version of this would be: 'The world and the objects in it display coherence and logic; and people act with reason'. Both parts of this second principle are necessary and dangerous to the child in equal measure. This must be of concern for parents and educators, and must inform their actions in relation to children. The important point remains that spellings are translations of one complex thing into another complex thing, from one mode to another: in this case the child translated parts of two letters written by the adult, the T and the H, into a new entity, the new letter TH.

The second principle might seem problematic in relation to fully competent adult spellers. How could I possibly maintain that any part of my spelling shows anything other than the mere re-instantiation of a convention? My argument is that there are so many different aspects to the entity that is to be copied that the principle holds. If you agree with my earlier point that spelling is in large part about language in its **visual** form, then it will be obvious at once that our adult spellings (as copies of written language) only ever attend to a few aspects of the visual form of spelling. Adult society has decided that many aspects of the visual form of writing do not need to be copied; but that decision is certainly not made public, it is not discussed, not mentioned to children, and it is a decision that could be revoked, should circumstances change. If I 'copy out' a quote from a book to use in my text, there is no expectation whatsoever that I should copy the shape of the type font in which the original appeared, or its spacing, or its layout, etc.

Or, to take another example, my handwritten comments on someone's writing may be difficult to decipher. But how could that be, except for the fact that the manner in which I reproduce the conventions of the roman version of alphabetic script is guided, precisely, by criteria of relevance applied by me, exactly in the way I have suggested. Of course, you might object that I have now slipped into a discussion of handwriting; while I would maintain that I am talking about aspects of visual spelling. But the same point applies to the spelling of sound. For instance, I have taken to writing *tho'* instead of *though*, and hardly anyone seems to mind.

The third principle goes to the heart of the notion of creativity, invoked in the title of this book. It says, on the one hand, that creativity is entirely usual and normal; and it says, on the other hand, that what is newly made is made out of already existing things. The proposal that creativity is usual flies in the face of the accepted myth of the heroic creative individual in Western societies, which for some 200 years now has insisted on the rarity of creativity, as the exceptional event, vested in rare individuals. I believe that the approach that I put forward here is an essential re-orientation. It will make us think in fundamentally different ways about children and their capabilities and actions. It is, I believe, both a much more plausible view – closer to the truth – and a necessary one for rethinking educational objectives and processes as they relate to the new demands of new social, cultural, and economic environments. In the era of mass production, of mass society, of mass communication, it may have been useful, essential even, to make creativity rare, and by implication make the vast majority believe in their exclusion from creativity – how else could mass production function? In the new era of increasing orientation to information-based economies, to lifestyle, to the niche or market, to constant innovation and change, that is no longer a possible view.

It could be thought that if all actions of this kind are creative, there would be no meaning left in the idea of creativity. I think, quite to the contrary, that it will force us to look at **kinds** of creativity, and at the social reasons for varying evaluations of different kinds of creativity.

The idea that everything newly made is both made out of what exists already, and is the effects of the interests and criteria brought to bear by the copier, forces us to look carefully both at what has been used and at what has **not** been used: that is, it makes us look with great care at the selections made by the speller. The interaction of what has been selected to be used with the speller's interest is what produces the new. Some examples of this are provided on pp. 122–25 (Example 3.13).

New-making draws and leans on what is available; and in so doing it has to stay close to the history of the culture, and close to convention. New-making also selects and adds; and in doing that it extends, changes and expands past history and present givens; and in that it challenges convention. New-making transforms the existing stuff in the light of the interests of the speller – and of course, within the limits of the freedom that convention allows. Clearly, some children, who after all already come to school as (or 'with') personalities, are inclined to stay closer to convention. Others are less inclined to do so. The fact that, inevitably, their interests

Example 3.12

Copying visual shapes: ideograms and letters

In all the examples of 'copying' that I have discussed so far, starting with the 'Thank you' (p. 60), one consistent focus is that 'copying' rests on what we might call **criteria of relevance**: you can only copy what you see, and you will see only that which is significant to you for some reason; and certainly you will represent only what you regard as significant. But 'significance' comes from your own interest, even though your sense of significance is likely to be manifold and complex. So the child, as indeed an adult, might say: ' I will copy this exactly as it is'. But at that point a whole range of factors intrudes: what I am told to focus on, what I like, what seems important and so on.

In copying the Chinese character for 'hands' (work done in class as part of a celebration of the Chinese New Year, when the child was 6 years old) there are a number of crucial things the child does not know: the principles of character formation, for instance (although the dotted lines are a means of helping the child); and the nature of the tools used to draw the characters. The latter, a seemingly trivial point, makes it hard to know the meaning – the significance – of the 'blobby' end of the strokes. Visually they are very prominent, and so they should be important; but they are, of course, the effect of drawing with a brush, and therefore to a large extent they are incidental or accidental (though significant in terms of calligraphy, the 'look' of ideographic writing). In the child's copies this becomes and remains an important feature at the base of the character. The relative lengths of the crossbars – the much greater length of the lower bar, for instance – cease to be a feature. Without an understanding of the principles, of a system of representation it is difficult to copy it. Is the curve of the vertical stem important? Is the inclination of the cross-bars significant? In the absence of that knowledge, the child supplies her own principles, which can, with some little effort, be recovered from her copies: 'This is some kind of J, with two additional crossbars', she seems to be thinking.

(Continued on pages 120–121)

Pure

once there was a girl
One there wes a girl

letany

Example 3.12 (continued)

The example on the facing page shows very much the same issue faced by the same child, some two and a half years earlier, in relation to her 'own' alphabetic system. Her mother had written – at the child's request – 'once there was a girl', which the child then 'copied'. Here, as in the Chinese system, it is clear that the child is searching to understand the principles of the writing system, of letter formation and of the relation of letters to each other. The *ce* of *once* is seen as a single unit; the *h* is reinterpreted as a vertical stroke with a linking line to the following *e*; and the model *a* (in *was* and *a*) is seen and reproduced as a single convoluted line.

This too is not copying, but reinterpretation and transformation guided by principle: not the principles of the adult, nor of the conventions of the system, but those of the child.

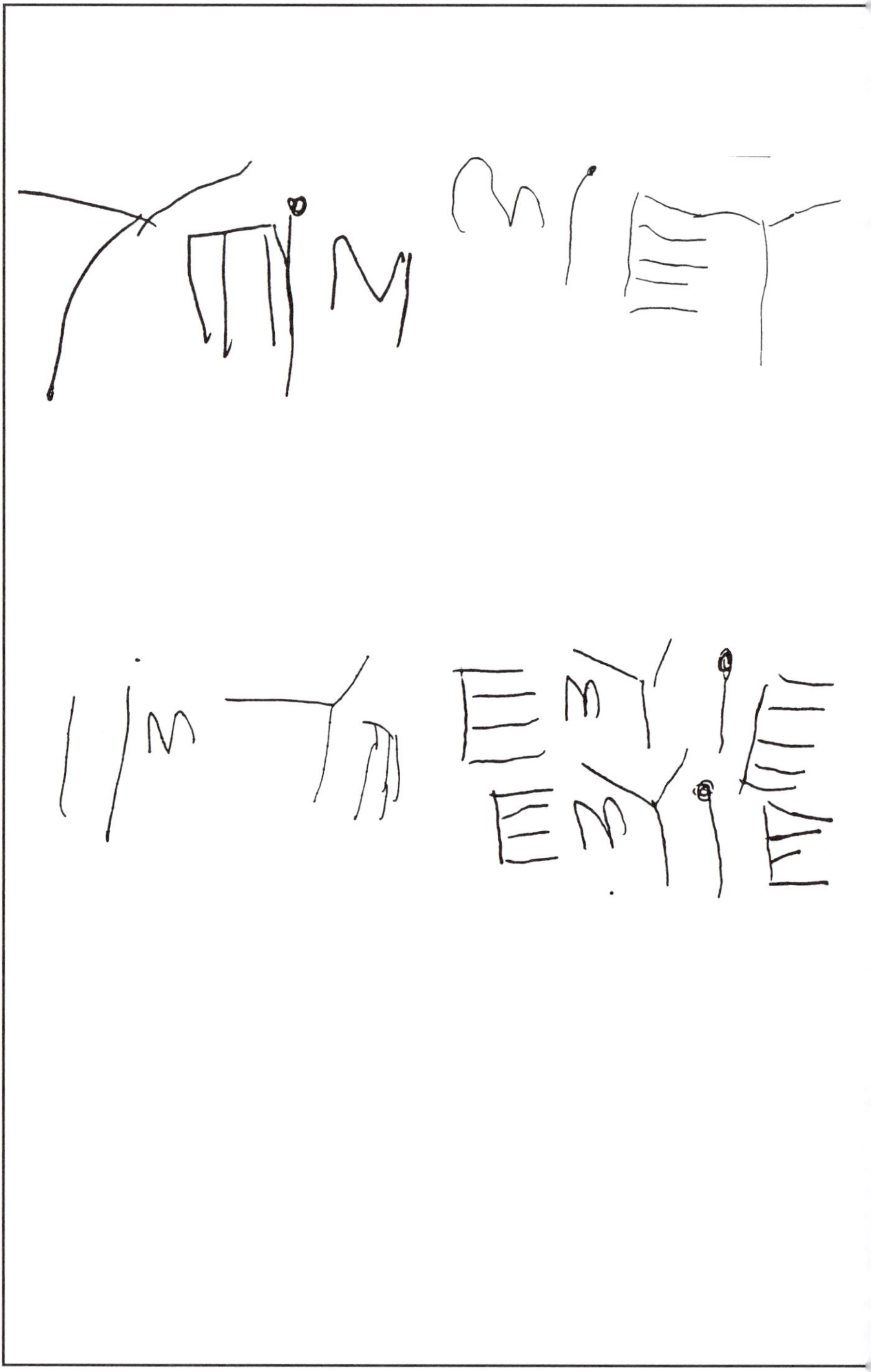

Example 3.13

Spelling: making the new from the old

The letters in Emily's name are given by the culture in which she grows up. This still leaves the child with the task of getting a sense of what the individual letters are, how many there are, what their shapes and spatial orientations are, and so on.

The letter that seems, on the face of it, to pose most problems for Emily is the letter *E*. But the *E* is not in principle more complicated in its shape than the *M*, or the *Y*. So the reason for the difficulty with the *E* may not be a difficulty at all, but rather that this is the letter that has the greatest affective charge for her. And so this letter can be the carrier of the enthusiasm, exuberance, energy that she feels about her own identity. She chooses an existing shape, with its meaning, and endows it with the additional meanings of her affective disposition. This is not to deny, of course, the point I made earlier, that there is also the question of 'numerosity', (of the distinction of 'many' and 'very many'). She could equally have used the *M* or the *Y* for the expression of affect, as the objects of 'decoration,' but there is no motivation for her to do so.

(Continued on pages 124–125)

Example 3.13 (continued)

This set of examples is quite different. It concerns the child's learning of symbols for numbers. Numbers must be a puzzling phenmenon for the child: they have 'names' like words do; they can be written out using letters (ie *3* can be *three*); and yet they have their own system of transcription. So one question for a child might be: what makes numbers different from letters? What is the principle that distinguishes the one set of symbols from the other? I do not know whether this question is ever asked, or what answer might be given, but in these examples that question seems to be explicit.

The first set of examples was 'written' by the child when she was 3 years and 4 months old; she said of it: 'This is the numbers'. Clearly this is an issue for this child at a very early age. The second set of examples was 'written' one year later, at the age of 4 years and 6 months. What seems to distinguish 'numbers' here, by contrast with a set of letters written some time between the two examples (at the age of 3 years and 10 months) is the irregularity – or difficulty – of their shape, in the early example; and the angularity, the 'linearity', regularity, of their shape in the later example.

Again, the shape of the numbers is given; and so is the shape of letters. How the child makes sense of that shape, what sense she makes of it, and how she distinguishes it from the similar yet different shapes (and meanings) of letters, is the issue. This is also the place where creativity happens: she needs to make a distinction; that makes her search for principles of differentiation; and that leads her to transform the existing shapes of her culture.

differ means that what they select and what they ignore will differ, and so in periods when convention is not strongly asserted, spelling will vary from individual to individual. We are taught to overlook just how much our spellings differ, how individual they can be and are. Spelling by adults in informal situations, such as in diaries, in informal letters, in more intimate occasions of writing, are instances where spelling can be 'individual', and used as a means for individual expression.

The fourth principle states, in essence, that form and meaning are, as near as can be, identical. Provided that we have enough information about the thing that has been copied, we can make reasonable inferences about the speller's meaning made in her or his new spelling. The new spelling gives us an insight into the speller's thinking. To go back to the 'Look I've done it' example used earlier, we know the shapes of a capital letter *T* and *H*; we also know that in a quickly handwritten version the two letters can be run together. That knowledge allows us to read the run-together form as two discrete letters. We ignore the linking lines; to us they are irrelevant and so we don't see them. By contrast the child's focus on the linking of lines gives us an insight into what she thought: 'If I link all the lines as in the thing I am copying, I will have a letter just as in the original'. The numerous bars on the letter *E* of *Emily* tell us that 'numerousness' was in the child's mind, perhaps in the form of 'a whole lot' contrasted to that of 'not very many'; though precision about the number of bars seems not to have been in her mind at all, it seems. As a matter of fact she never produced *E* with fewer than three bars.

These four principles taken together allow us, indeed force us, to move away from a notion of mere copying, and provide the theoretical underpinning for taking these 'inventions' as seriously as I suggest we need to do. They give us insight into the child speller's (or the adult speller's) thinking, into their **interest** at the moment of spelling, and provide means in this way for new understandings of learning. They make creativity and innovation the centre of attention in all meaning-making, and they include spelling in the range of practices through which we all make meaning.

3.3 Form as meaning; meaning as form

The four principles that I have just 'spelled out' insist that form is meaning, and that the forms in which meanings appear are an apt expression of that meaning. This is a strange statement to make in Western cultures in this century. It flies in the face of the commonsense view that form and meaning are arbitrarily related: that there is no inherent or intrinsic relation between a particular linguistic form and its meaning. Let me give two examples that tend to be used to make that point. One example points to the fact that the 'same thing' has different names in different languages – *chien*, *dog*, *Hund* all name a domesticated animal of the canine species. The fact that different sound sequences can be used as names for the same entity demonstrates, so it is asserted, that sound (sequences) and meaning are arbitrarily related. This is the argument attributed to Ferdinand de

Saussure, who taught at the beginning of this century at the University of Geneva, and whose *Course in General Linguistics* was produced as a book by students of his from notes they had taken in his lectures. Another example that is often used is that of the game of chess. Say you had lost a chess piece – a pawn perhaps. You could say to your chess-playing partner or opponent: 'Oh, not to worry, let's just use this button here'. You could then both continue playing. This seems to confirm the case that form and meaning are arbitrarily connected: a button can take the place of a chess piece. But say you had lost, by some strange circumstance, four pieces, three of them black and one of them white, a pawn, a knight and two rooks. Say you had, by luck, three black buttons, of different sizes, and one white button. My guess is that you would use the smallest button for the pawn – the least valuable piece; the middle-sized button for the knight; and the largest for the rooks – the most valuable of the three types of piece that had been lost. My guess is also that you would use the white button to replace the white rook.

What you would have done would be to make form (in this case **form as physical size**) aptly match the meaning (the value of the piece): the smaller the value of the piece, the smaller the button, etc. Or take as another example the two designations I have just used for the person with whom you were playing chess – 'partner' or 'opponent'. Do you think it matters what you call him or her, 'opponent' or 'partner'? Does it change my relation if I switch from '**partner**'to '**opponent**'? I think that each term reflects a different perception of the relation, as **you see it**, that you imagine exists in the game. If you think it matters whether you call the other person partner or opponent, then you assume, as I do, that form and meaning are aptly related.

What is the point of this brief theoretical excursion, and why should it matter? If you think that spelling is a matter of trial and error, randomly engaged in, and then finally learned by the rote application of rules, then indeed it doesn't matter. But that entails that we have decided that there is nothing here to be understood, neither about the spelling nor about the speller. But if you want to see in children's early spelling the traces of their interest at work, then it is precisely this assumption that you need to hold. If you want to see in children's actions the traces of intelligent minds engaging with the world, then there is something here to be understood. Let me give two quite distinct examples (3.14 and 3.15 on pp. 129–31) to make the point that, to the contrary, there *is* something to be understood.

Take the case of the next example, 3.15 (pp. 130–31), writing in Braille. Do we assume that the child had no well-shaped intention, no interest, had not thought carefully about what the relation is between form and meaning?

My point is clear, I hope. In the chapters that follow I shall exemplify some of the kinds of interests that child-spellers have in the variety of examples that I will discuss. I think it will reveal the range and the complexity of children's spelling, their attempts to come to terms with the complexity, and I hope it will reveal something of the insights we can gain from taking the trouble to look at these spellings seriously.

oLL day AND oGL NiGht

A littLe Bord had A Grat

BiG frit-

1) Ropabe yoget

2) Cnem Fne Sh

3) Shozden ok Lamb

4) potatos

5) Crunch pent butten

6) blanchd anmens 25c

Example 3.14

This example comes from a 'workbook' in which the child collects all kinds of things: collages, stories, drawings, maths exercises, (on the cover it is called *Book of Maf's)*, and so on.

What is there to be understood in this spelling? It seems to have been a poem, and the carefulness of the handwriting, its careful 'roundness', the swirl on the letter *y*, all point to what I have earlier called 'a heightened style', but here expressed in the visual aspects of handwriting. This 'aesthetic style' contrasts with the 'everyday schoolbook style', where she writes carefully, but without that extra flourish; and it contrasts with her 'everyday style', as shown in the shopping list, with its exaggerated casualness.

The heightened style extends to the spelling of the sound – the *oll* – makes that sound 'rounder' and 'fuller'; the *o* of *bord* ensures that the vowel is sounded fully.

The spelling of the *look* of writing is of one piece with spelling of the *sound*, and tends in the same direction. What is spelled here is meanings of a certain kind. We can ignore them if we choose; we could say that calligraphy belongs to handwriting; and we could say that 'oll' is mispelled. But, if we do so, it is at the cost of mistaking the child's use of spelling as a complex means of making meaning.

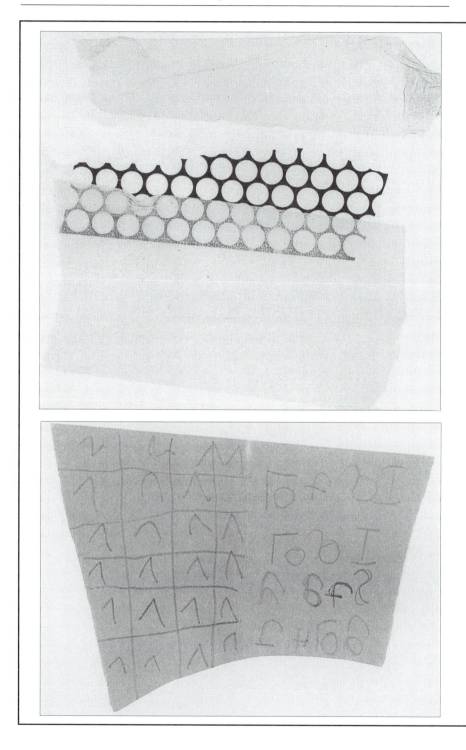

Example 3.15

Braille: making meaning through touch

For the last discussion in this chapter I have chosen two examples that illustrate the child's highly developed, and quite abstract, understanding of spelling as the representation of meaning.

The first is an object, folded paper, stuck together at one end to form a kind of envelope. Stuck onto this is a piece of pink, perforated, metallic tape. When asked what this was, the (then 4½-year-old) child said: 'This is a bag. This is a ticket-purse; when you go on holiday put all your tickets in there.' When asked about the tape on the front she said that it 'is letters for blind people saying what it is – only when you close your eyes'.

The second object, a small piece of blue, firm paper, folded in the middle, was 'a story'. When asked 'What's this?' about the grid on one side, the child said, 'It's for blind people to feel'.

Here the degree of abstraction is, if anything, greater than in the first instance: it is, first, a transduction of the written story to the abstracted version of Braille, and then it is a transduction from the medium of the perforated tape, which **is** accessible to touch, to the representation of that as an abstracted system. This represents one 4-year-old's understanding and awareness of spelling as a meaning-making system. Whether as a parent, educator or academic, I would like to be at least as sophisticated in my understanding.

a libol Powim

I love my dad
I love my mum
I love mu brither
bub most of ole I love my famiy

Example 3.16

What gets spelled is the issue. Among other things – the conveying of the young poet's feeling about her family, for instance – there is clearly the question of spelling 'beauty' or 'beautiful feelings'. A number of features are used all at the one time to achieve this: the careful layout, the careful 'drawing' of the letters and words, the careful 'scoring' phonologically of how this poem is to be sounded out, performed, (the spelling of 'powim' ensuring that the word has to be said with great deliberation and care; and similarly with 'ole' and 'brither'), the visual images adding their meanings: flowers beautifully arranged, 'hearts' coming in an unbroken stream from the lips, and, in the original, the colours chosen for the images.

For the child poet there is likely to be no differentiation between these; each is as important as the rest, and each makes an equal contribution to the meaning overall. It isn't that the child has to learn to transcribe all the meaning that there is to transcribe, and to do so accurately: she already does that. The task for her in learning to spell is to choose what meaning to leave aside in her spelling, to learn to ignore what her society tells her is not really relevant.

Of course, there is a bit of tongue in cheek here too: but then irony has also always been a part of the poet's armoury.

Chapter 4

What do children try to spell?

4.1 The boundaries of spelling: making a mark to make meaning

In the first three chapters I began to show the variety of children's interests that is revealed by a closer, serious and empathetic look at their spellings. In this chapter I want to draw some necessarily artificial boundaries around forms of spelling. One overriding question is: 'What is spelling?' What do we include or exclude from our view, from the domain of our investigation?

Let me put this question in a concrete form. In cultures with pictographic, ideographic or logographic writing (there is no agreement on the terminology, as each term focuses in a significantly different way on these writing systems) – in Chinese, say, or Japanese – the units of the writing system, the characters, do not stand for sounds in the way that letters do, but stand for ideas or concepts – whether as a word, or as a smaller or larger element of meaning than a word. In Example 4.1 I give several instances of this.

Clearly, such systems are **writing systems**; they allow language to be recorded, and stored, and disseminated. But this is not a recording of the sound of the language – not a recording of language-as-sound, but a recording of language-as-ideas. Ideographic writing records ideas. Is this spelling?

Our answer to this question has profound consequences. If we say 'No, this is **not** spelling', we are left with one, very narrow, definition of spelling. If we say 'Yes, it is the recording of language and therefore it is spelling', we are left with a different, much broader, definition of spelling. If we adopt the broader definition, we have committed ourselves to accepting that language-as-ideas (in contrast to language-as-sound) can be represented by images – just so long as there is agreement about what the symbols are, and how they are to be used. In principle we can then also accept that language-as-ideas can be represented by other symbol systems: by gestures, by objects or surfaces which can be touched and felt; and so on.

This question is not merely 'academic', as the unflattering phrase has it. It is important largely because children adopt this as their position on their making of marks in the world, as their representation and recording of their meanings.

However much we may eventually need to wean them away from such a way of thinking, the fact remains that this is their starting point; and I want to insist that however much we succeed in our attempts to bring them into the logic of the alphabetic system, this initial logic remains with them – and therefore with all of us – for all of our lives. Some of us learn the new logic very well, and that initial disposition gets covered over by the logic and the rationality of the alphabetic culture; for others – such as the vendor of the *cyclemen* – it remains closer to the surface, able to activate, and to motivate spelling-as-meaning even in alphabetic cultures.

One serious consequence of the adoption of the alphabetic logic is that we learn to overlook the other transcriptional, recording systems that we use, or which some or many of us use: systems that organize the possibilities of expressing meaning via the movement of the body most strongly as in gesture languages, but even less strongly in the less codified gestures that all of us use in everyday communication; expressing meaning via the organization of sound as music, which is regarded as expressive, but not as articulate, 'rational' communication; expression of meaning via touch; and so on. The case of gesture language (usually called 'sign-language' as in American Sign Language, 'Aslan', etc.) is instructive in illustrating the consequences of the narrow approach to spelling. Until very recently (the change is as recent as three or even just two decades ago) severely hearing-impaired children were taught to use their hands to spell – that is, to shape the letters of the alphabet – despite the fact that their communities had a fully articulated representational system for expressing ideas, namely the various sign languages used in those communities. One central factor, perhaps *the* central factor, in the broader community's unwillingness and refusal to accept sign languages as 'real' language was the fact that many of the signs in these languages do, like the characters in pictographic scripts, 'mime' the meanings that are being expressed; that is, they rest on the logic that says that language is first and foremost about meaning, and these meanings can be represented in gestural configurations. In the commonsense of Western linguistics this logic excluded the systems from being considered as proper, full human 'languages'.

In this chapter I am concerned with three related issues. The first is that of the 'boundaries' of spelling. What do we regard as being clearly a part of spelling? What do we think of as being outside spelling? The second issue is that of establishing the range of things that children do spell (according to our definition), and what meanings are made by them in those spellings. The third issue is the matter of the abstractness with which children approach spelling, as indeed they approach all things and events in their world. The reason I am interested in this third issue is that it shows beyond any possibility of doubt that we must treat children's spellings seriously if we are actually interested in what they are about, and if we want to develop plausible ways of teaching them spelling in the conventional sense without adopting merely authoritarian methods.

In this chapter, and in the two following, I shall use a relatively conventional interpretation of 'spelling', something like: 'the representation and recording of

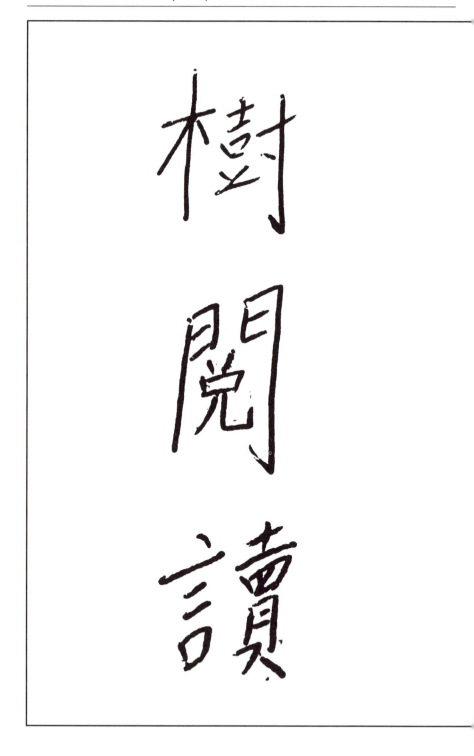

Example 4.1

The character *tree* is an ideophonetic character, which means the categories of the character are a combination of a semantic component and a phonology component. Its semantic radical is *wood*; the other part is the phonological component, which gives sounds for the character. In this case, it happens that the phonological component also provides meaning. As the sound is the homophone of *stand*, the meaning is thus borrowed as well. Therefore, for the character of *tree*, we could say it is a kind of wood that stands still and tall.

There are two characters for the word *reading*. The first character of *reading* is combined with *door* and another component inside. It is also an ideophonetic character. However, when we look for the original meaning, it is closer to the meaning of 'call the soldier' than to 'reading'. It means: 'the general counted and called the names of soldiers inside the door.' It might be some kind of ceremony before fighting.

As for the second character of *reading*, it is combined with an element of *speech* and the other, which is not *sell*. For centuries the right-hand component has been confused with the word *sell*. In fact, the top of the component is different from *sell*, as it is a short line followed by a long line, instead of a long line first as in *sell*. It is now that the right-hand component could not be properly explained. We could just get the meanings of this character from the semantic radical and know that it is an action of explanations by speech to interpret what you have read.

meaning through language by means of the letters of the alphabet'. Even this narrow definition leaves some blurred edges, as I shall show in this first section. It does, however, draw a quite firm boundary between all those innumerable objects made to represent the meaning of something or of some event, and 'the representation and recording of meanings through language by means of the letters of the alphabet': for instance, objects such as a folded, sticky-taped, drawn-on, three-dimensional paper. I am thinking here of things such as a 'computer plus mouse'; or, another such object (made at a younger age), a 'choo-choo train'. These are left out of consideration from here on. 'Objects' such as those in Example 4.2 straddle the boundary. They have some of the characteristics of the computer or the train, and some of the characteristics of spelling in the narrower sense.

When I say that I draw a boundary, this is not to say that these objects do not need to be understood in the context of what spelling is. To a 4-year-old there is, I feel, very little difference between representing one bit of their world by making a three-dimensional object, or another by making a two-dimensional drawing – whether of a model of a *Tyrannosaurus rex*, or of some lines of print. From the adult's point of view there is every difference: while there is no code for representing *a computer plus mouse* as a 3D object, there is such a code for representing a sequence of words in a specific order; and this, among other things, accounts for the adult world's present preference for language.

Often the 'objects' made by children are very close to the more straightforward world of spelling and yet retain some object-like character. In Example 4.2 there are some examples that exist on this blurred boundary.

One real problem around spelling is precisely that of the boundaries: who draws them, and where. Adults draw them in one place, and turn that into the rules of rigid convention; children's interests lead them in quite different directions, perhaps even into having no boundaries. It is unlikely that children think of language and meaning in anything like the same fashion as adults do. The kinds of meaning that children (try to) spell are often entirely unlike anything that the conventions of the adult world could allow for – even if we stay within the realm of representation with letters.

Taking a broad conception of spelling as our starting point not only allows us to see what children do spell, where their interests take them in this aspect of making meaning; it also allows us to see more readily what has been ruled out of being spelled by the conventions of the adult world. In the early spelling of children, **spelling meaning** is what spelling is.

4.2 What gets spelled?

An instance of 'spelling meaning' is shown in Example 4.3. Unlike earlier examples, where the child seemed to have focused on the *look* of print or of lines of print (for instance, Examples 3.2 and 3.3, pp. 88–91), here the intention seems very much to 'say something'. Writing/spelling is about meaning, and the meaning that is attributed to the writing/spelling is not necessarily the literal meaning that the letters spell out, as Example 4.3 shows.

In Example 3.10 (pp. 108–111), I showed a child's spelling of rock-n-roll music – a transcription of sounds, of words and of a melody heard by the child. This is spelling as transcription, from the medium of sound to the medium of letters. In Example 4.4, the child produces – generates – her own 'song'. This is not a transcription of something heard. This is a case of the production of a text rather than of transcription; spelling here is making visible, and it is the recording of an internally produced text. Something that exists in the child's head is given outward expression and form.

In Example 4.4, the resources of letters are used in an unconventional fashion, though it is important to recognize that such uses, while they may be unconventional, are not unusual. Writers of children's books, novelists, advertising copywriters and many others use letters in this way entirely as a matter of course: no one accuses them of misspelling, a sign that the rules are tight in certain areas and not in others, and tight for certain people and not for others. That of course is a subtle matter, not 'spelled out' anywhere, and very difficult for children to discover.

Example 4.5 shows some of the features of spelling of Example 4.4 (and also of the rock-n-roll song, Example 3.10, pp. 108–111). This, however, is not a song, but a piece of dramatic writing, complete with background noises, sound-effects, etc.

The issue of transcriptional systems and what they make possible and what they make difficult or impossible is at work in many different ways in the early spelling of children. It is the issue in many of the examples discussed already, for instance in the acrostic poem, or in the rock-n-roll song. Here I want to discuss one other type of example, and one other issue, the 'mixing' of transcriptional systems, before moving to the third section, where I shall focus directly on the abstractness of children's thinking about spelling and the matter of codes. The set of examples in 4.6 concerns the 'spelling' of numbers. As I said in Chapter 3, numbers must seem a very odd phenomenon for a child: they have a 'name', like other 'things'; the number 3 has the name 'three'. Numbers are sound-words like other sound-words such as *tree*; and numbers are meaning-words such as *many*, *few*, *some*, *lots*, all of which express 'numerosity'. But the number 3 is also spelled within its own transcriptional system, which makes numbers seem like letters; the symbol for the letter *O* for instance, can also be the symbol for the number *nought* – or is it *zero*? (*Nought* is in fact more word-like than *zero*, even in its etymology: 'ne aught'/'not aught'). But whereas words such as *tree* are spelled with several letters, a word such as *three* can be spelled with a single 'letter', *3*. That makes numbers odd indeed, in that a whole sequence of sounds is 'spelled' by a single symbol. For a child this must be quite an unsettling factor in their thinking about spelling rules more generally.

In fact there are peculiar rules for the 'spelling' of numbers in adult conventions. Publishers have quite specific rules about this. In running text, numbers below ten are usually written as words; with numbers above ten it becomes less

Example 4.2

Spelling of things in the world

The recipe for making Prune Splits (?) (invented by this 8-year-old cook) not only spells the names of the ingredients, but 'spells out' a set of instructions at the same time. These are in part 'spelled' by the verbs in imperative mood: crush! cut! mix!, but they are also 'spelled' by the sequence in which ingredients and procedures are laid out. Mix is last, as it needs to be. The full meaning of the recipe is spelled out by all these aspects together as much as by the words and their spellings.

What is spelled out here is the genre of a text, with all its criterial features, and with all its component parts.

The book is an object made by a (nearly) 4-year-old. On the front cover is her name; the two inside pages shown here (the page folds to produce the front page, the two inside pages, and the back page (which is left unused). The 'written' text is 'This was a little girl who had a brother called . . . .' What the child is representing/'spelling' here is *book*, the object; but she is also spelling the image–text relation of the inside pages, as well as the actual 'written' part of the text.

I assume that for her there is no real distinction between spelling as 'spelling of written language' and spelling as the representation of image and written language. Nor is there necessarily a distinction of image, text and the object (and genre of) the book. Spelling here means 'the representation of the most significant aspects of the object being spelled'.

The third example 'This is the ticket what says "Emily" and I can go to France with that ticket', shows a similar conflation of spelling the material object, spelling the text-as-genre, and spelling as the production of writing in the usual sense. Both in the 'book' and the ticket, criterial/material features are spelled: the **pages** of the book, and its image–text relations; and the size and shape of the ticket, as well as the materiality of the ticket – it is made from quite firm paper, suitable for being a durable ticket. The book has the author's name spelled on the front; the ticket has the name of the owner of the ticket.

All three 'objects' are objects that belong to the world of writing, and it is that which makes me think of them – and infinitely many others like them – as existing on, as straddling the boundary between, spelling in a narrow sense and spelling in its most extended sense.

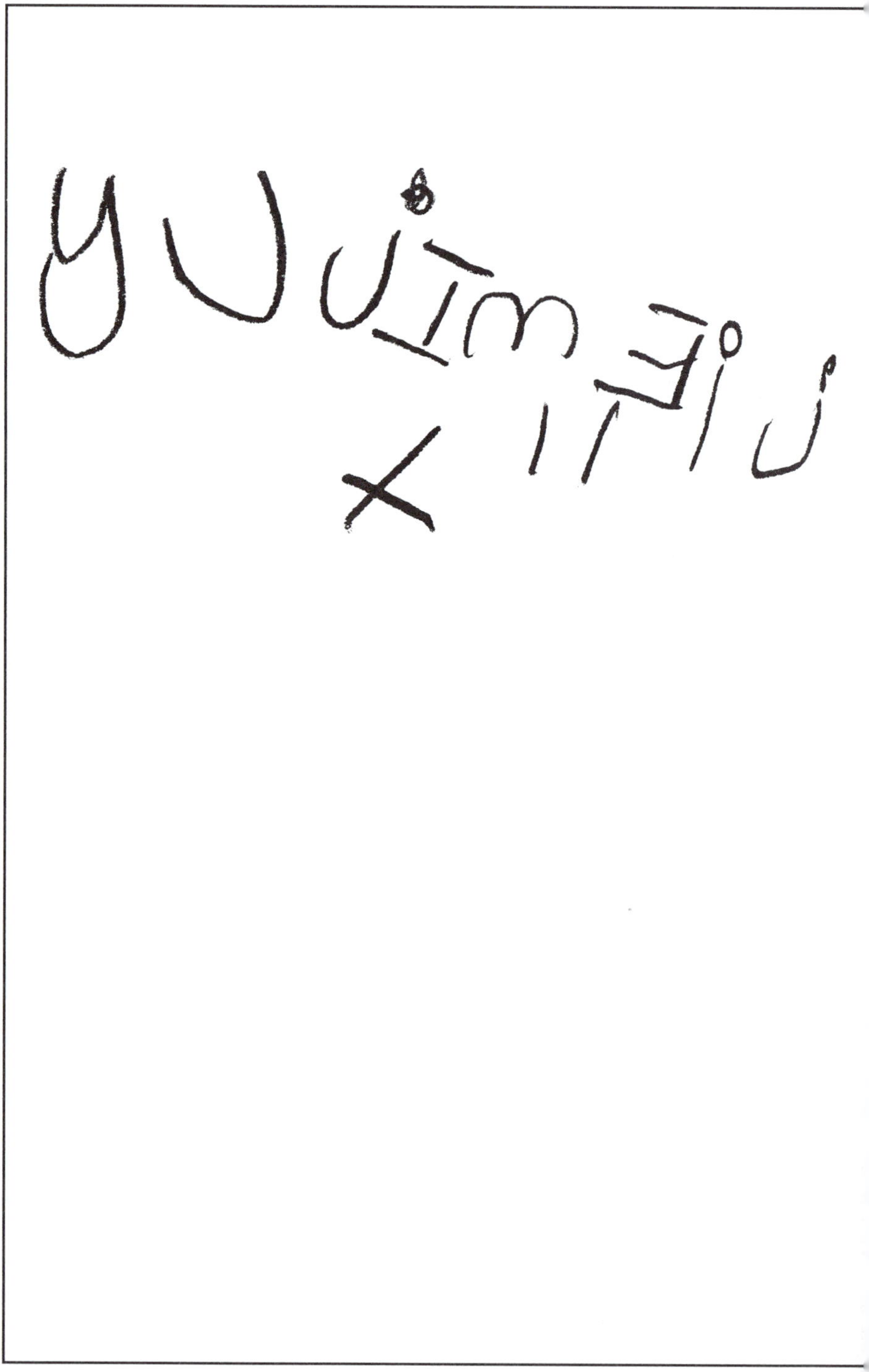

Example 4.3

Spelling meaning, spelling as meaning

This is a letter; it was delivered with the comment 'Here is some writing for you'. The text itself was read out: 'Maybe when we go back to France I might still be 5'.

For this (nearly 5-year-old) writer, spelling/writing is about making a meaningful message: that is the meaning of print, clearly. It is unlikely that the child at this stage makes any distinction between spelling and writing; writing is about putting meaning into visible marks, so that they can be transmitted to someone. That meaning of spelling (writing) is likely to adhere to (writing) spelling for a long time, perhaps always – even for highly literate adults.

In fact, what the child had written was her own name and that of her mother, from right to left. I am sure that she is completely aware of that, and yet she attributes to that 'writing' the small message that she reads out.

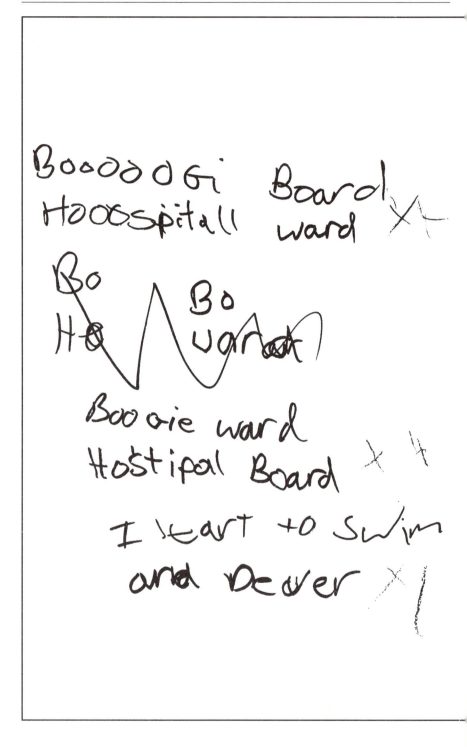

Example 4.4

Spelling sound and rhythm

The representational resources of letters are here used to record a song, composed by the child. This is not a transcription of a song previously heard, but a new song, made of course out of the child's knowledge of such music (there was at this time a Glen Miller revival, as well as one of the frequent rock-n-roll 'revivals'). She uses letters to spell words; to spell sounds, indicating the length of vowels by the reduplication of the letters *o* (to produce the long vowel u:) and the duplication of the letter *l* to indicate emphasis.

Rhythmic features are also spelled by means of letters, namely through spelling the short syllables *bo, ho*; and these short syllables form a short, rhythmic interlude.

The long drawn-out vowels of the first two lines (repeated four times) may also indicate melodic features, and the undulating line across the second set of two lines may be an indication of the melodic movement–but that is speculation. What is clear is that vowel quality, vowel length, intensity of pronunciation of a consonant, rhythmic features, and perhaps melodic line are all 'spelled'. They are significant features for the child, and therefore are important to be spelled.

bom ~~flolibx~~   flash owo
no saved evvey one of
us. he's a mitee vord of
the world of gras. wooo
bom 6X. Flashboow1 what are
you ~~Michael~~ dowing magret (open fire)
zizzizziw. (what do you
~~Michael~~ ~~mean~~ hes stil a live ciw him)
emiwy
bom x6. (ow flash you a
savewer. can i have your
otirgriaf ~~bow~~ ow flash you
saved the erth) mte you
siwnce

Example 4.5

Spelling dramatic performance: 'writing things out'

The question for the child here is 'How do you spell/transcribe a dramatic performance?' She is not aware of the adult conventions, though it is also clear that the adult conventions overlook, ignore or write out many of the features represented here: 'write out' both in the sense of 'being written out of the text, 'disappearing', and in the sense of written out as words, in the form of stage directions.

Here it is clear that the child has a specific problem with the transcription: some of the sound effects are attributed to a source – one of the actors – and some are not. In other words, the questions for the child are: 'Where do background noises come from? Who or what makes them? Who do I attribute them to?' However, what is clear is that they are part of the script: they are not written out in either sense of the words. What is also clear is that adult versions do write such things out: the 'zizzizziw' might be 'written out' as a stage direction 'sounds of flames spurting', but here it is made specific; similarly with the 'wooo bom' etc., which would be written out as a stage direction 'crashing noises off'.

The question 'What gets spelled?' is here clearly at issue for both child and adult.

'The mighty lord of the world of grass'
(normalized version)

Sound (off):	bom (×6) flash, owo
Voice:	He saved every one of us
	He's a mighty lord
	of the world of grass.
Michael:	Wooo bom (×6)
	Flash woow
	What are you doing, Margaret,
	open fire!
	zizzizziw.
Emily:	What do you mean he's still alive,
	kill him
Sound (off):	bom (×6)
Voice:	Ow flash you are a saviour.
	Can I have your autograph?
	Ow flash, you saved the earth.
Minute silence	

certain whether to use number symbols or letters. No one, however, writes 'In fourteen hundred and ninety-two Columbus reached islands near the coast of central America'. In other words, the line between a number as a word like other words (say, ten), and a number as a member of a quite different transcriptional system (a different **semiotic** system), is a relatively fluid one; it is a line that isn't clearly drawn. Of course, that simply makes problems greater for children.

Children seem to recognize from quite a young age that symbols for numbers have a different look from those of letters. In Example 4.6 the manner in which that difference is handled by a child (between the ages of 3 and 5) is illustrated and explored in some detail.

My last example in this section is quite closely related to Example 4.6, but in a subtle way. The spelling of numbers raises the issue, in a way, of two competing transcription systems. The word or number 'three' can be spelled either with a numerical sign, *3*, or with letters, *three*. Both transcription systems are perfectly adequate to deal with the concept three. Of course there comes a point when the limitations of one system begin to appear: not just as in my example of spelling 'fourteen hundred and ninety-two' (on cheques that I write I have to represent 'a figure', 'an amount', both in letters and in numbers), but particularly when I want to do calculations. If I want to add four hundred and sixty-two to eighty-nine, it is easier for me to represent it as $462 + 89$. Our systems of calculation as taught in schools are built on numbers being represented in that form. That shows up a fundamental point: transcription systems are not neutral – they have inbuilt limits and advantages. It is important to bear this in mind at all times, especially when looking at children's spellings, because their early spellings are attempts by and large to get beyond the limitations imposed by the transcriptional system of the alphabet, by the limitations of the letters. Children's spellings always attempt to do more than letters will easily allow.

Example 4.7 shows a real mixing of transcription systems, that of the alphabet, Chinese characters, and images. The question with spelling always is: What transcriptional systems does the child have available to her, or to him?

4.3 The abstractness of children's spelling

In this last section I focus on the remarkable degree of abstractness that is evident in many instances of children's spelling. It gives a clear insight into their grasp of just what is involved in translating – spelling – something recorded in one transcriptional system into another. It is a cognitive and conceptual feat of a quite astonishing kind.

Some of these spellings/translations are deceptively simple in their appearance. Example 4.8 is a case in point – rhyming slang, typically associated with 'Cockney' English.

The complex but playfully hidden 'spelling' of rhyming slang is much more directly visible in Example 4.9. I have already discussed Braille, in Chapter 3 (p. 130), but it is worth considering this case once more.

Both 4.8 and 4.9 involve (at least) a double translation: and, in that, both involve a highly abstracted understanding of the activity of spelling, as involving the use of and movement between codes. It also involves a very subtle understanding of the possibilities of shifting from perception through touch to the possibilities of perception through sight, or hearing; or the understanding that there can be playful and complex relations of one code and another, and the meanings that can be made. But the perception of the transcriptional system as a kind of code is crucial. It is this that makes possible an intellectual gain of enormous proportion: the understanding that from this real, physical thing, I can get to this abstract conventional thing, and back again. This is what gaining a sense of control of one's environment is built on.

Properly and fully understood it enables a child or an adult to invent codes that will control any part of the environment. Both magical incantations and the elaborate edifices of mathematics are built on that same understanding. In my next example, 4.10, several of these things are involved: it represents the invention of a code to capture and control, and to replicate movement. Once the code is created, it has the potential for creativeness: new structures, new texts, new events can be envisaged, designed and if, wanted, performed. The world can be changed.

There are many other instances that illuminate and demonstrate the abstractness of spelling: for instance, the use of spelling as a mnemonic (which seems to me a quite common motivation for the consonantal spellings, as in the Christmas cracker example, p. 114, and many others); or the abstract organization of the attempts at an acrostic poem. However, the three examples discussed here do, I hope, make the point that I wish to make: the great conceptual, cognitive, imaginative effort involved in children's early spelling, and the degree of abstractness that they achieve, effortlessly. As someone interested in education I am convinced, of course, that we need to be fully aware of this if we want to develop forms and methods of teaching spelling that treat children with the care that the intelligence displayed in their spellings so clearly shows; or, if beyond that, we want to know what these young people are actually like and what they can do.

Example 4.6

Spelling of numbers

(a) Children seem to recognize from quite a young age that numbers are different. This 3-year-old (3 years 4 months) said 'This is the numbers', as she showed me what she had drawn (written, spelled). She is aware that there are such things as numbers; and her drawing seems to indicate, by comparison with letter shapes that she drew at a roughly similar age (3 years 11 months), that she is aware of a difference in shape. What seems distinctive, if one can make inferences between the shapes and what the child was thinking, is the change in drawing/writing direction that number symbols require. This is a matter that seems separate from the spatial orientation of the number symbols. Spatial orientation is a problem, as it is with letters (see Example 2.14); but change in writing/drawing direction seems not to be a problem – or not so clearly, with letters.

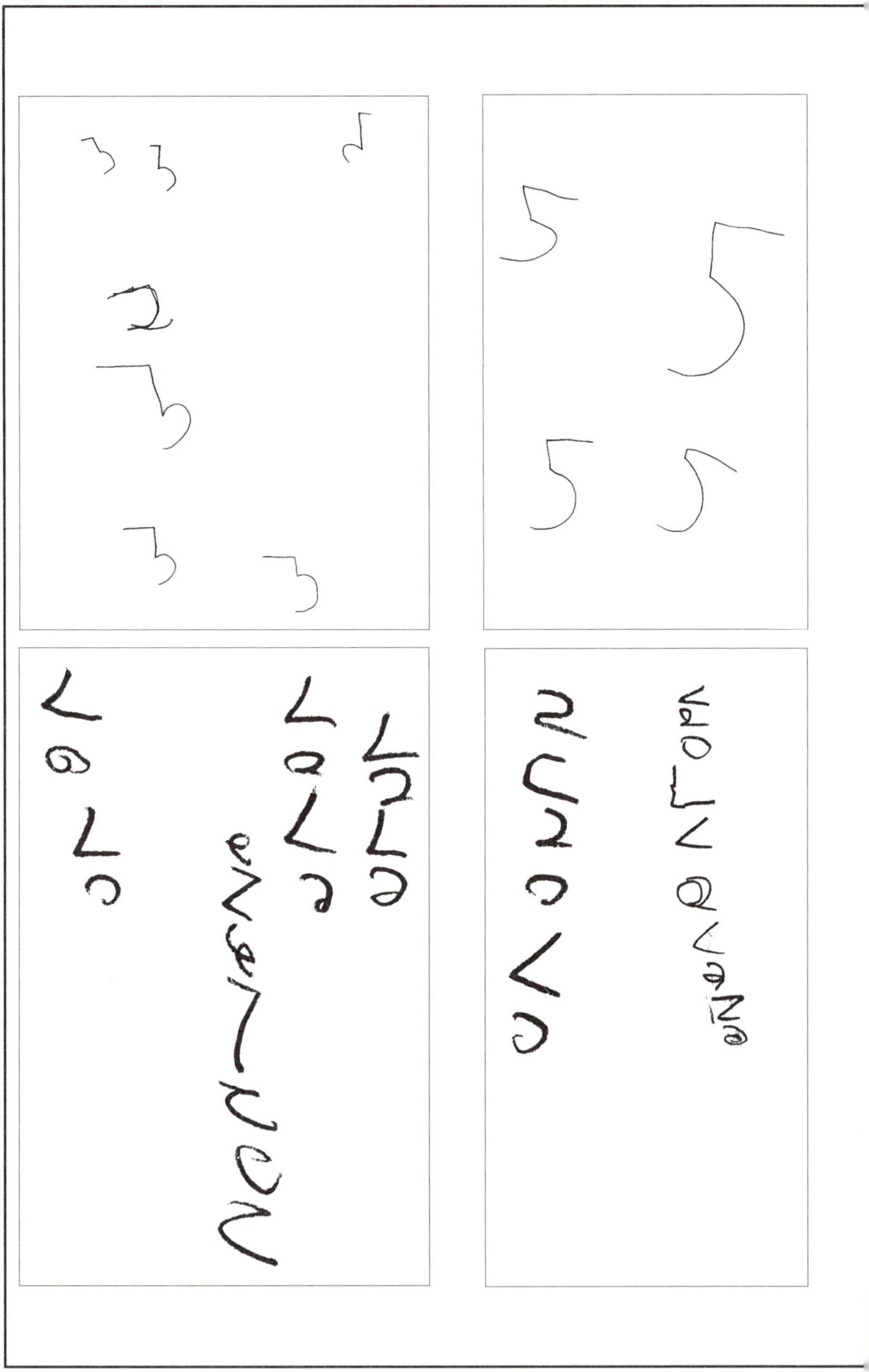

Example 4.6 (continued)

(b) The problem of the drawing direction is clearly **the** issue in this example, made some six months later than (a). The drawer's/speller's/writer's comment was 'This is when I was practising the number 5. First I did it wrong, then I did it right'. I asked 'Why was it wrong?' Her response was 'Cause I went the wrong way'. At that point she picked up my pen and drew the number that is the darkest here, the number in the centre, most like a 2. A day later she produced the four examples of a 5, on the second page of what was a folded sheet.

(c) Roughly a year later she remains interested in 'numbers' as a distinct phenomenon. Several distinctive characteristics seem to have appeared: the 'angularity' of some numbers, perhaps the number 7; the 'circularity' of others, perhaps numbers such as 6 or 9 and a 'number' such as 0; and the combined circularity and angularity of numbers such as 2 and 5.

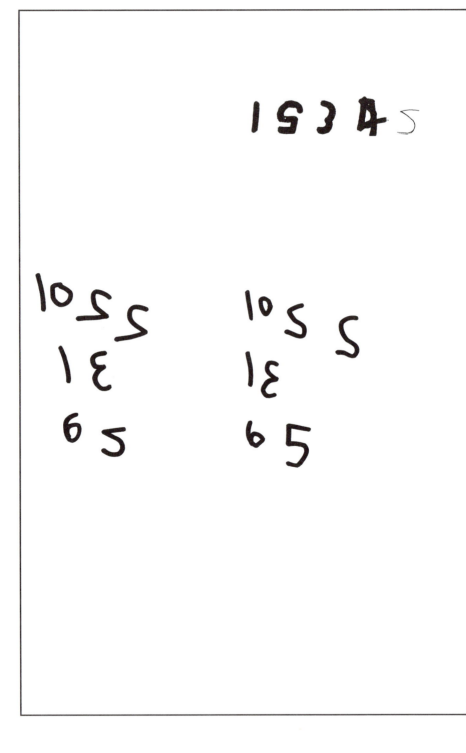

(d) Eight months later (at the age of 5 years 1 month) the number shapes are relatively clear, though spatial orientation remains an issue. There are still blurrings of shapes, as between a 2 and a 5.

(e) The spatial orientation of letters presents one among the many puzzles of writing/spelling, as earlier examples (for instance, the spelling of Emily; Examples 2.12–2.14), show. However, the letter *E*, whether oriented to the right or to the left, remains recognizably the letter *E*: in fact, it remains an *E*. As long as we remain alert to the visual aspects of spelling (and my analysis of the printed sheet produced by the Teacher Training Authority, showing the consequences of ignoring that, is there as a warning), there is no real problem.

(f) The last example comes from the environment of the school. On the sheet, from an exercise book, is an example of practice in the shape – and directionality – of the number 5. In the lower left-hand corner is evidence of the enormous control needed by a child to manage directionality, especially when it seems to go counter to the 'natural' direction.

With numbers, however, spatial orientation matters, as the example here shows. So what looks in some ways as though it were the same phenomenon, spelling numbers and spelling with letters, differs in this important respect; and children have to learn that difference. In that sense numbers are closer to images than letters are, closer to drawing than to writing (there is no equivalent of 'running writing' with number symbols).

Cheung Ka Hei (1), P4D   5th March, 1997

[turtle drawing] and rabbit race

before the story, [turtle drawing] and rabbit have a race. The race first is [turtle drawing], second is rabbit. Because rabbit 去了 sleeping. This story is [turtle drawing] and rabbit econd race.

This race 終點 is the river. The race 開始了. First, rabbit is the first, but it behind the river, it doesn't running. Because it ~~doesn't~~ doesn't swim. of the hour, [turtle drawing] 追上了. He swimming to the river. of half, one 鯊 fish want to eat ~~him~~ its. rabbit 立刻 swim ~~to~~ after [turtle drawing]. The 鯊 fish jumped to the [turtle drawing] Rabbit 立刻 swim to the [turtle drawing]. He helps hits but 鯊 fish chases them. Rabbit fast swim to river 的另 one 邊. 帶鯊魚 doesn't eat them. [turtle drawing] said "Thank you, rabbit." 於是, [turtle drawing] and rabbit 做了 good friends. The story 完了.

Example 4.7

Mixing different kinds of spelling; mixing codes

The examples here come from a Hong Kong primary school, where 10-year-olds are learning (to write) English. In some examples, the young learners stick to using the alphabet. In others, they switch to a transcriptional system that they know much better.

In this example we see a child going one step further still: the alphabetic system is mixed with Chinese characters, but in addition this writer has used images (of a turtle) to represent one of the two central characters.

I assume that for all the writers there is no question but that they are writing a story, and their ready switch from one transcriptional system to another seems entirely unproblematic. (The examples were written outside the quite formal demands of the classroom, where such mixing would not be allowed.) In doing this the two young writers show two principles that we all employ, or want to employ: to use the transcriptional system to the limit of its and of our own ability; and when that 'runs out', to make use of other transcriptional systems. It is an entirely normal response, and all children employ it.

This example may seem extreme, but I believe it simply shows in heightened form what all of us do – or would wish to do if we felt less constrained. The use of gesture to fill in for speech when 'words run out' is of course one such example; and there are many others.

Some questions remain for me. It seems to me that in using the image of the tortoise the child thinks: a tortoise looks like this; the image of a tortoise will do to represent the idea of tortoise. And he may have thought quite similarly about his use of Chinese characters: the ideas I need here look like this; a whole idea is represented by a whole character. Does, or can, a child who thinks like this see letters in the way we, who came from alphabetic cultures, do?

Example 4.8

Complexities of spelling: rhyming slang

Emily's class had discussed rhyming slang, and this seems to have made a real impression on her and her friends. Over the days following I discovered several other examples made by them in the context of different games.

By everyone's admission, rhyming slang is 'clever' and it is complex. It involves, usually, an actual rhyme, of the 'headword' of the phrase that is said, with the 'head-word' of the (hidden) phrase, which is being spelled. In other words, rhyming slang is a kind of puzzle, in which the clue lies in the sound: similarity of sound of the **spoken phrase** suggests the sound of the unspoken phrase, and from there it suggests the hidden meaning. At times there is also a kind of 'semantic rhyme'– a pun: *trouble and strife/wife*. That is not the case here. In this case the child needs to understand that similarity of sound (and of rhythmic pattern, of syllable pattern, of sound shape) will provide the clue to the sound of the intended phrase, to the phrase that is being spelled, and to its meaning.

What is entailed in (spelling) rhyming slang is the understanding that the sound pattern of a phrase that means one thing (or is non-sensical) can provide a clue to the sound pattern of a phrase that actually means what is being spelled. It is an intellectual feat of considerable magnitude: in its complexity it defies any simple-minded explanation of spelling as being about sound–letter relations. Of course, the verbal play involved opens up aesthetic as well as cognitive possibilities of a vast dimension. But it also reminds us of the cognitive complexity – and playfulness – of all spelling.

For those unfamiliar with 'rhyming slang', the phrase being spelled is: 'I went to Hampstead Heath'; the phrase from the 'spelling system' is: 'I went to clean my teeth'.

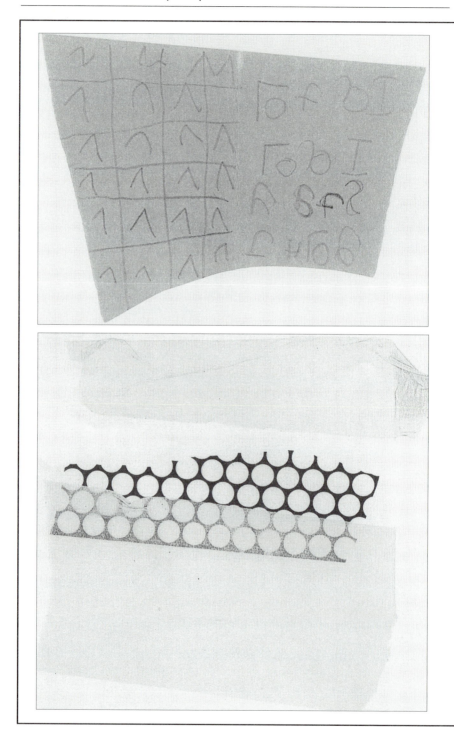

Example 4.9

The abstractness of children's thinking about spelling

I have already discussed this example (in 3.15) together with the 'Braille tape', but it is worth reflecting once more on the processes that underly this spelling.

This object/text is a book. It is made from quite firm blue paper, about 10 cm × 5 cm, irregularly shaped, probably a bit of paper left from some previous cutting-out. It is folded to make the book, with a front page, the two inside pages (shown here) and the unused back page. On the front is the author's name and a drawing of a tall flower, standing in grass.

The child's comment to me was, 'This is a story.' When I asked 'What's this?', pointing to the grid pattern on the left-hand 'page', she said 'It's for blind people to feel.' Like the example of rhyming slang, this is a double translation, a complex spelling. First the 'story' is spelled, translated from sounds to letters set out in lines, neatly. This story is then translated, spelled again, into the grid pattern. To judge by the speller's comments, this grid pattern is itself a translation ('It's for blind people to feel') from the touch-able to the see-able; it translates the regularity of the **look** of Braille into a purely visual pattern. It abstracts from the superficial visual irregularity of the symbols of Braille to the regularity of the system of Braille, which the child has perceived correctly; and it translates from touch (and sight) to sight alone – as though this abstractness would still leave the script per-ceptible to blind people.

3.p.rr.d ⅍. ⑤   F.p   N.ɔ) 4·x

ʸ —|x²ˣ 》

⌈⌈ — rise ୪ run

〉 — Petty 8hetasc

》 — head ᵘᵖ head ˡᵒʷ

— |X — avcross paton

PS — prepartion for sotay

N.ɔ) — new Pawlker

·P — pasesion

a — avrabes

⅍. — jump

ɔ) — spin around

Example 4.10

Spelling the meaning of movement: how children make up codes

This invented code is a means for describing (some of) the steps of (classical) ballet (as learned in the very early stages); and, once invented, it is used by this child as a productive system. The lines at the top of the page describe a brief 'passage' (afterwards performed by the child as part of a larger performance).

There are many points of interest: for instance, the invention of a 'grammar' that allows her to make longer sequences, sentence or paragraph-like. The symbols in the code itself have varying characteristics. Some are simple abbreviation: *ps* = (preparation for sotay); *p* = *pasesion* (position); *a* = *arabes* (arabesque). Some symbols are mimetic: that is, they mimic the movement that is being spelled – for instance, the symbol for *spin around* – but also, less obviously perhaps (and somewhat more abstractly), the symbols for *head up head low*, *across paton*, *jump*. The symbols for petty chetase mimetically indicate the position of the feet.

Others, such as *rise & run*, seem to use an abstracted version of the initial letter of the words that describe the action.

In this example, as in others I discussed in Chapters 2 and 3, it is, of course, essential that she should already know the distinct elements (the 'steps') that she wants to spell; just as it is important for the child to learn the words of a language before they can be spelled.

In all these, the child draws on what is available in her symbolic world; and all of the symbols are meaningful, even if in very different ways. In other words, the means for making meaning that are available to the child are freely drawn on in order to make a new code with which to 'spell' the thing that she wants to spell; and in order to make her new meanings, as in the passage at the top.

Chapter 5

The look of spelling

The confusions around spelling run deep. Anyone who feels that spelling is one clear thing, and that the rules of spelling can be quite clearly produced, is deeply misguided. Spelling is many things. It is best to acknowledge that that is so, and then deal with the facts of a very complex phenomenon.

Take Figure 5.1, a page from an exercise book from 4–5-year olds in the English school system. The page has been photocopied and stuck into the exercise book that deals with writing and arithmetic.

I have made the point in earlier chapters that, in order to spell, it helps to know the written version of the language. We can rephrase that now and say that, in order to spell, it helps to know **the look of the language**, to have a visual image of the units of the language, mainly of words and of letters. To that extent spelling is a visual/visible punctuation, a framing that separates off one signifi-cant **visual** unit from another. In the early attempts at writing by children this absence of clear frames, this lack of punctuation, is a major problem for them. Of course, framing can only happen when we know what is to be framed; and ditto for punctuation. Many of the examples that I have discussed earlier show this quite clearly. Example 5.2 is another example.

The 'look' of a word can help to settle the question of its internal shape and coherence. In a situation where the spoken form of a word may fluctuate from one moment to another, a child's reliance on sound will lead to difficulties. Children are acutely precise in their analysis of sound, so inevitably one accurate transcription of a word heard in one moment is overthrown by another accurate transcription of a pronunciation of that same word the next moment. In that con-text a settled look for a word can be a great help. Example 5.3 shows the doubt of a young speller about the sound/shape of a word.

The example in Example 5.3 points to the fact that the spelling of words rests on an understanding of words as visual units: which is precisely the point of the page from the exercise book in Example 5.1. In that page there were two versions of words, one the visual unit produced by sequences of letters, and the other the visual unit of the **picture** of the thing at issue – the lion or the lamp. At this point I want to draw attention once more to the fact that the route of spelling of picture-as-word is a real possibility for children at an early age, and they seem to see it just that way. They seem to experiment with the possibility of a visual lex-icon, and in this they come up against difficulties that are not unlike those with an alphabetically produced lexicon (Example 5.4).

It is worth pointing out that, as in many areas of social life, children do not (yet) have a settled sense of the shape – concretely or abstractly – of the social world. For instance, while I may find, when I puzzle about a spelling, that the look of a word does not feel right, a child cannot of course know that. The writer of *Satday/Saturday* cannot draw on a settled sense of what that word should look like; and so for a while she has to continue to experiment.

The visuality of language, its look, has other consequences. If, as often hap-pens, I type *langauge* on my computer (a mistake common for many of us), it is the appearance of language in a visual/spatial dimension that has gone wrong, and it is its visual appearance that tells me that something is awry. I still pronounce *langauge* in the way I did before; and I still **know** how it should be spelled. What has gone wrong is the sequencing of letters in writing it out – **not** the sequen-cing of sounds in speaking it aloud (or saying them quietly in my head). Something has happened in the translation from sound to sight, from the audible to the vis-ible. There are any number of reasons for this: in English the **sound sequence** *ua* is unusual (unlike Romance languages, where this sequence – as in *linguaggio* for instance – is entirely usual). Because the sound sequence is unusual, the let-ter sequence is also unusual; and therefore the link from my brain to the muscles that I use in typing or in writing is not really grooved for a sequence such as this. The sequence *au* occurs much more frequently, again visually, in words such as *beautiful, laudable, caustic*, and so the link from my brain to my hand is used to such a sequence: it is grooved to producing this.

Children do not yet have this grooving. In a very real sense they are not used to anything at all. The whole world is new for them, comparatively speaking. So for them the translation from sound sequence to letter sequence is something that has to be learned, has to be established. In their learning they use such help as they can, and if sound seems to suggest itself as helpful, then they will use sound. In Example 5.5, I show four examples of this difficulty.

These examples show a quite normal state of affairs: it is produced by the need to translate from one kind of order – from the temporal sequence of sound – into another kind of order – the spatial arrangement of letters. If the visual spelling of *night* requires the order *g h t* that is fine, but it is wrong to assume from that that the sound sequence is like that. It is in this translation, in the transduction from the visual to the aural/oral, that problems arise for some children, problems that can be labelled as **dyslexia**.

Children solve the problems posed by their world in quite different ways. One issue that is entirely related to visuality and display, or to arrangement of ele-ments in space, is that of directionality. I have discussed this in Chapter 2 (see p. 67). For some children, such as Emily in Example 2.14, it is a real issue. For others, it is simply passed straight over, seemingly, either because it is immedi-ately recognized and understood, or perhaps because it is 'accepted' by them,

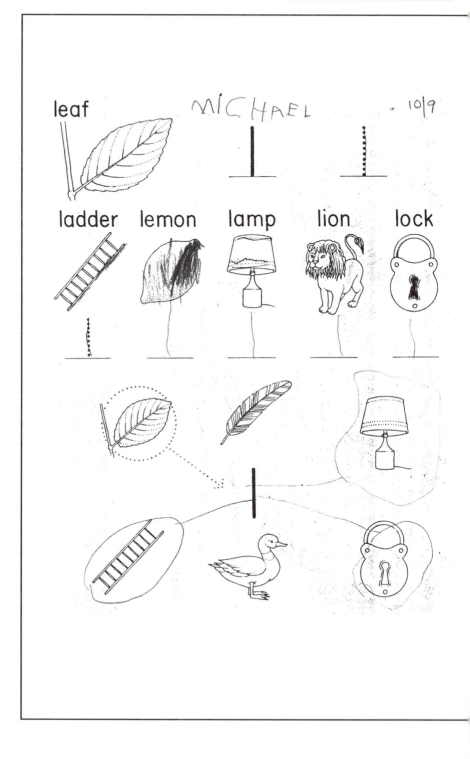

Example 5.1

The complexities of spelling: words, letters and images

The focus of the page is the letter *l*. It is shown as the plain graphic symbol; it is associated with printed words beginning with *l*; these words are themselves associated with the images which the words denote. The visual word *lion* is associated directly with the image of a lion. The word here is as much a visual entity as is the image, and this is the origin of one of many approaches to reading, where words, even though they are represented with letters, are treated as visual entities, and recognized as whole entities.

In the exercise in the lower half of the page the task is to connect the images, whose words start with the letter *l*, with that letter in the centre of the page. The assumption may well be that children will 'say' the word and hence associate the letter with a sound. There is, however, no real reason why the children can't remain focused on the visual symbols. Of course the teacher will get the children to *sound out* the words and the letter. But the point remains that all the complex issues of spelling are there; with a predominance of and emphasis on language (and spelling) as visual. On this page sound is backgrounded. Spelling is shown as a visual matter.

WaSa Pontir eth
e n Wo

Once   upon   a   time   there
was   a   69 go t
big   giant.

Example 5.2

Spelling as punctuation and framing

The child is familiar with the phrase 'once upon a time', too familiar perhaps, so familiar that for him the whole phrase is one 'fused' unit. In fact, judging by the spacing *wasa* may also seem to him to be one unit, as is *pontim*. The clarity of the teacher's version by contrast has distinct framings and punctuation by space: the notion of words as visual entities is clear.

The word as a unit of sound is often difficult to discern; one sound 'runs into' another. Hence the word as a clear, distinct visual entity is helpful for a learner of a language, whether child or adult. The spelling of a word puts the focus on the external boundaries, and on the external frame, as well as on the internal coherence of the word. The visual framing of words puts focus on the distinctness of one word from another.

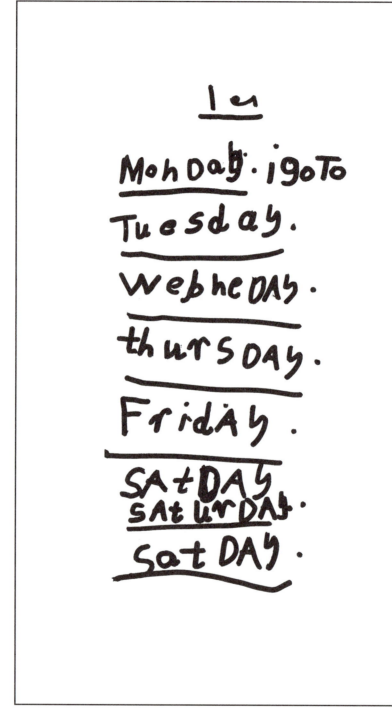

Example 5.3

The look of spelling

How often do you look at a word you have just written, and say to yourself 'That doesn't *look* right'. Equally, I often find myself looking at what others have written, and find that something doesn't *look* right. This happens particularly frequently when I read the writings of young people, older school children, or undergraduates in particular. When I see 'independant' it *looks* wrong to me. I then say it 'in my head', and decide: yes it should be 'independent'. 'In my head' the visual memory of the third *e* in the word has translated itself into a sound-image; I try to say it with an *e*, which of course is impossible for anyone else to hear.

Of course that points to the fact that there is a constant pressure for change, even on the conventional forms of spelling; my bet would be that in another 30–40 years no-one will bat an eyelid over 'independant'! The occasional headlines 'Official: undergraduates can't spell!' above articles chronicling such changes in exaggerated fashion are always a good indication of the direction in which spelling changes are moving.

However, my main point here is to emphasise this matter of the look of spelling. I verify my spellings visually; if I have a doubt I say the word in question 'in my head', trying out the difference in sound, and look. This example is, I think, such a case. The child has accurately transcribed the sound she heard; she then *looks* at what she has written, and a doubt emerges: this doesn't look right. She then writes it out to look right. But the right look doesn't match the evidence of her ears, and so she goes back to what feels right in terms of what she thinks she has heard, and its transcription.

In time she will learn that in matters of spelling a paradoxical situation applies: *look* is more important than *sound*. This is so because writing is permanent, therefore it is more stable, and in consequence it is more conservative. But sound, and its ceaseless dynamic, is what eventually produces the change in look, with children and young adults leading the way – aided occasionally by advertisers and other creative users of the look (and sound) of language.

Example 5.4

A visual dictionary?

The two kinds of examples both point to children's experimentation with the idea of pictures-as-words, in a way which goes beyond their usual drawing or painting as representation.

The first two examples are produced by two children quite independently of each other. Both are the result of a school visit to the British Museum in London. Both children were clearly impressed by the façade of the Museum and both used the same word to describe it: 'a cliff': One wrote: 'I went to the museum, and there was a cliff'. 'That's the cliff,' said one. Neither child knows the word 'façade' and so uses the nearest suitable word that each of them has – *cliff*. That is a creative act in relation to language. But, it seems, there is an equal problem in relation to their 'visual lexicon': neither of them has an item in their visual lexicon for 'entrance formed in the manner of a Greek or Roman temple, with huge columns and portico'. That is, neither has available some visual icon such as that which is available to the maker of a tourist guide to ancient sites, or to a cartoonist or to someone producing a quick sketch. Both children lack the ready-made verbal form; but equally they also lack a ready-made visual form.

(Continued on pages 176–177)

Example 5.4 (continued)

My second set of examples is one of many of this kind which I have observed children make. These are, in my view, the equivalent of visual words: here it is of 'the little girl in different moods'. They are usually drawn as here, (or cut out) on small pieces of paper, so that they tend not to be part of a larger entity (part of a drawing, or 'story') but are separate, moveable, entities, *tokens*, in the way that words function as tokens. They can therefore be used in different ways, in different contexts, just as a word can.

At this stage (the figures were drawn at the age of 4 years 11 months; the drawers of the 'cliff' were both six years old) children seem to take it as a given that ideas can be 'spelled' either as words or as pictures. In most cases they have neither the lexical nor the visual 'word' available, and so they have to make up either of them. If you don't know what a 'facade' is, the problem of verbal or of visual expression is really quite similar: you have to be metaphoric. And so the visual spelling is just as 'incorrect' as the verbal, even if the expression either verbally or visually seems highly appropriate.

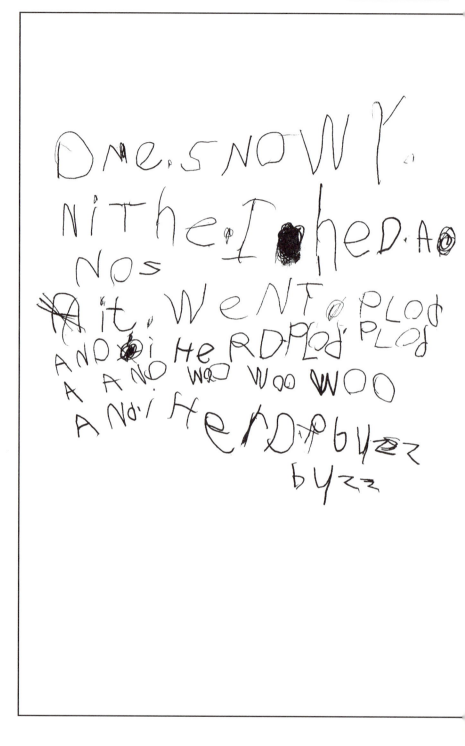

Example 5.5

Visual sequences

The 'snowy night' story was written in school; by a five-year old. The class had previously been given a sheet on which they had to connect words like *plod, drip, buzz*, with pictures of dripping trees, plodding feet, etc. His spelling of 'night' as 'nithe' shows the difficulties of handling complex sequences of letters – he has the *h* and the *t* of *night*, and the difficulty of accommodating a spelling rule which he seems to know, namely that *e* at the end of the word 'lengthens the vowel before' – or however the teacher may have explained that relation. He places *t* before the *h*, I assume because in *sounding* the word he can clearly hear the *t* following the vowel, and he has no particular reason for placing the *h* before the *t*. The *h* is there because he has *seen* it when he has seen the word written before. There is no reason for the presence of *g* or the *h* in the spelling of contemporary standard English, other than that of history: in Chaucer's English they would still have been pronounced (as it is in the German equivalent *Nacht*).

(Continued on pages 180–181)

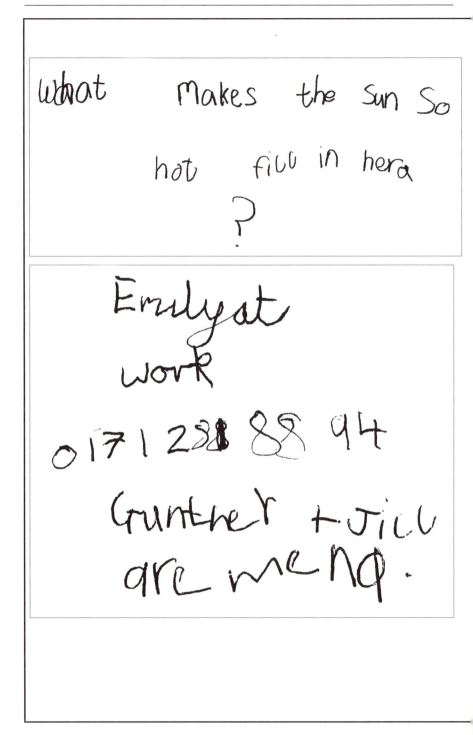

Example 5.5 (continued)

There are similar problems with words such as *Tuesday*, spelled by one 8-year-old as 'Tuseday'. 'Tuseday' is in fact a well-motivated spelling; it follows words such as *use, excuse, fuse*, in which the sound is, for many speakers, very close to that of the *ue* in *Tuesday*. Again, because this child may have seen *use* much more frequently than she had seen the *ue* of 'Tuesday', it is understandable why she follows that spelling. The look of *use* is convincing; *ue*, like *ua*, is not a usual letter sequence in English, and therefore not often seen. The *ue* in Tuesday also has a historical explanation: that of the name of one of the Gods in the Nordic/Germanic pantheon.

The sequences *mena* and *yera* seem to me to have a dual explanation. On the one hand in the local dialect spoken by the young inhabitants of the school to which they go, a word final *a* seems obligatory for many words: at the end of *ok, yes, here*, etc. is tacked on an a-like sound, with a sharply falling intonation, indicating impatience, annoyance: ok*a*, yes*a*, her*a*. *Visually* the sequence of *cvcv* may seem more plausible to the child; and, in terms of the sound of the words, the child may feel that the word-final *a* has the effect of lengthening the vowel in the preceding segment, much like the *e* in words such as *flame*.

unproblematically. In Example 5.6, there are some examples of children 'solving' this problem in two different ways.

Visuality, and the use of space, enables spelling to mimic what 'the thing spelled' is like. I have mentioned this several times already, though only in passing. I want to focus on that aspect of spelling now, in talking about the **aesthetics** of spelling. We know of course that there is calligraphy, and we know that, in Chinese and Japanese cultures particularly, this is developed to an art form. What is at issue is the use of graphic means to 'spell' beauty: to make the thing that is spelled appear beautiful through graphic means of representing.

In many discussions this is what is meant by the term 'iconic' – to make the representation actually **be like** the thing that is represented in some essential ways. Let me first give two relatively straightforward examples of iconicity, the letter *s* drawn by a 5-year-old, and a picture of a spider, drawn as part of the same exercise (Example 5.7).

Example 5.7 illustrates the notion of iconicity: the fact that you can use the representing medium to represent important aspects of the thing that is represented. Here I want to draw attention, on the one hand, to the fact that this is a totally usual and normal strategy in making meaning. It is what is usual – it is the norm – even though the commonsense and the theories of this century have largely insisted that this is not so. On the other hand, I want to focus on one particular aspect of spelling in this connection: using letter shapes, and other visual aspects (spacings, size) to 'spell' beauty, or loveliness, to signal a 'heightened sense' of look, of sound and of feeling (Example 5.8).

Spelling as visual activity is quite generally recognized, though what is usually meant by that is that we have a visual recognition of the shape of words – that we treat whole words as quasi images. Through this book I want to expand not only our notions of what spelling is, but also of what can count as meaning, and to show the two as entirely related. Spelling *that which is beautiful* is as much a part of the making of meaning as is the spelling of what we regard as the definitional aspects of the meaning of the word *cat*. If we do not acknowledge that, then it is we and our theories who are the poorer.

Example 5.6

Directionality in visual spelling

One aspect of visual spelling is 'directionality': the child has to discover and learn that there is a writing direction. I have discussed this earlier (see Example 2.14, p. 67) in relation to Emily's learning to write her name. Here I want to show that different children employ different strategies, probably because they 'see' the issue differently.

In the first example, the child had asked a nearby adult how to spell 'register' (as in the register kept at school). She wrote down the letters, one at a time, as the adult spelled them. The initial letter *I* is most likely the child's trancription of the hesitating 'ahm' that preceded the actual spelling out of the first letter, the *r*. But the point of interest for me here is 'directionality'. The child starts at the left and moves right; when the child came to the end of the line she simply 'turned the corner', as it were, and continued, now writing in the new direction, from right to left. (This is the manner in which Ancient Greek was written, 'boustrophedon' – 'as the oxen plough'). However, the individual letters remain oriented from left to right. In other words, the child has two distinct notions of directionality: one for the direction of writing and one for the orientation of individual letters.

In fact, this is an example precisely from the period when in writing her name she had begun to turn back from writing from right to left, to writing from left to right. Abstractly and cognitively the two principles are not yet sorted out by her. This is, therefore, an example right in the middle of a transitional phase.

(Continued on pages 186–187)

Example 5.6 (continued)

The second example (by the same child) is also written 'boustredophon': turn the corner (or, 'come to the end of the field') and turn round and go in the new direction. But this time the letters of the name written from right to left are oriented in the same direction as that of the writing direction. If the writing is from left to right, so are the letters; when it turns to right to left, the letters 'turn around' as well.

In both these examples the child has no problem with sequence – the letters are in the 'correct' sequence; and no problem with linearity – the letters are all in a line. The issue is directionality.

The next two examples were written by a different child, at about the same age, around 5 years. The child had written a little 'story' in his school exercise book: 'I went to the airport' (underneath a partially coloured-in drawing of the event). He solves the problem of directionality differently: when he comes to the end of the line, he does not 'turn around', but continues on the line below, and writes in the same direction as before, with the letters 'correctly' oriented.

At the same time, and on a different page in the same book, the child had completed a number exercise ("3 and 3 → 6"). Here the directionality, the orientation of the number three produces a 'wobble': even though the child writes the 3 correctly on all pages where numbers occur *by themselves*, here I assume that the fact that he is *writing* makes him treat the 3 as a kind of letter, and its directionality is that of the writing.

Sometimes the experimenting and sorting out which I have shown here are seen as signs of a real problem, of a pathology; and the word 'dyslexia' always hovers close by. I think it is essential to insist on two things: these experimentations (and the various differing solutions adopted in the process) are entirely normal. They provide insight into a child's enquiring and puzzling engagement with the world. They are also signs of the attempt to sort out the shift from the logic of sound to the logic of space. For some children that remains a problem, for any number of reasons, perhaps because their own fundamental orientation is more to sound than to space, or more to space than to sound. A recognition of the level where the problems lies is the essential prerequisite for any attempt to provide real assistance for these children.

Example 5.7

Iconicity: making the letter be like the thing

The relation between the look of a letter, that is, the letter as image, and the sound to which the letter points, or for which 'it stands', is, to all intents and purposes, arbitrary. We cannot say that a *g* sounds like the sound for which 'it stands' – as in *Gill*, or that as a *j* – as in *Jill*, 'stands' for the same sound. But the urge to try to find a real connection – to see the letter as in some way iconically representing the sound – is always present. I might try to say that *o* mimics the shape of my lips (or my mouth) in making the sound, or that *l* mimics the flatness of my tongue in pronouncing the letter; that letter-sequences such as *sl*, as in *slide, slime, slip, slop, slurp*, etc., are mimicking the sound, and that the sound mimics a 'feeling' about these words. This is the subject of phonaesthetics; and it has given rise to much speculation, and more derision, on the part of 'serious' scholars. It also gave rise to intensely serious occupation, particularly in the seventeenth century, to devise a universal alphabet based on the shape of the mouth, lips and tongue in speech.

Nevertheless this urge is there, and I want to say that it is there because that is how we make and take meaning. For children it is absolutely taken for granted. The two attempts to give an explanation for the shape of the letter *s* on the page opposite (drawn/written by a 5 year old at school), are testimony to this urge; and to this fact of meaning-making.

The shape of the snake, an example mentioned before, mimics the shape of the letter *s*, and the other way around; this letter *s* is clearly drawn to be snake-like. It also sugests, with the drawing of the tongue, the hissing noise of the snake, mimicking the sound which 'the letter makes'. This is therefore an instance where there is a double iconicity – in the visual dimension, and, suggested, in the dimension of sound.

The spider presents a more difficult problem for the child; here he has to suggest that the body of the spider is curled up; and here the letter *s* is drawn to make that parallel seem clear – this is not the snake-like *s* that accompanies the picture of the snake. The long tail of the spider might be meant to suggest the spindly legs of the spider.

The '*s* as in square' example clearly presents a problem for the child. The object neither looks like nor sounds like an *s*. Yet I think that the child has attempted to mimick the square-shape in the *s*, by turning the curl at the foot of the *s* into a shape that might be seen as at least distantly resembling a square.

In all three instances, but particularly in the first two, iconicity is strongly at work, making the thing which is represented seem or look or sound like the thing that represents it.

Flawase

I Pike the Flawase
From my gadin i tone areawd
and Sbop to See the

Yelow Vose I go to Pike wine
a thone gest Stik in my figir

Example 5.8

Heightened style: Spelling beautiful shapes and beautiful sounds

Is Calligraphy part of spelling? The conventional answer would be 'No, it doesn't spell anything; it just looks nice in itself'. This answer rests on a narrow conception of language, roughly of language being 'about' rational, articulate, explicit meanings; and from that point of view spelling is the means of capturing just that aspect of meaning through the medium of letters. But we know – no matter what grammarians, linguists and others might say, that much of the meaning of what is said lies in *how* it is said: exchanges of the kind 'Yes, but what did I say?' 'It wasn't what you said, it was *how* you said it' are familiar to all of us.

I want to accept that children have a much wider, more open, more generous, more encompassing notion of meaning; and therefore of spelling, and of what it can do.

In the poem 'I pick the flowers' both the letters and the images are equally carefully drawn; both are 'spelling' the beauty of the objects, and the intensity and the heightened character of the feelings. This is a style adopted by this young speller/drawer (she was 6 at the time) whenever she produced a text in which she wanted to stress the beautiful look and feel of the text she had written.

(Continued on pages 192–193)

Translation

Flowers

I pick the flowers
from my garden I turn around
and stop to see the
yellow rose I go to pick one
a thorn gets stuck in my finger

a libol Powim

I love my dad
I love my mum
I love my brither
dub most of ole I love my famiy

Example 5.8 (continued)

But she is not just interested in a beautiful look; she is equally interested in a heightened style in sound. I have included the title of another poem 'A litol powim' because I think here it is particularly clear that she is 'spelling' a specific kind of sound. This spelling is quite systematic. In *litol*, the use of *o* ensures that the otherwise weak vowel (which often is 'swallowed') is actually pronounced fully and carefully. The same is the case with 'powim', where the spelling ensures that both syllables are fully pronounced. The variation between the sounds indicated by *o* and *ow* on the one hand, and the *i* on the other give a marked vocalic contrast. The full emphasis of both syllables in *litol* and *powim* ensures that both words are said with due care and with a greater duration – they are lengthened. In this poem, there is no haste; there is care in articulation; there is deliberation in every respect.

The same is true of *Flawase*. The young poet ensures that all syllables are fully and carefully pronounced – in saying the poem we feel ourselves lingering over these sounds. In the letters she chooses to represent the vowel sounds there is again this care for variation in sound; ensuring that due weight is given to each sound – hence the *stik*, where the high vowel *i* contrasts with the duller vowel that is actually there in *stuck*.

This very careful spelling of sound – spelling out what the sound should be – seems to me entirely within the range of things we call spelling. But if it applies to *sound* then I think it can apply equally well to *look*. In both cases, what is at issue is the attempt at spelling meaning of a certain kind.

Chapter 6

The sound of spelling

6.1 The nature of talking

The English word *language* is related to the French word *langue*, tongue. In many languages the ability and the 'gift' of speech is named after the chief organ used in speaking, the tongue. So 'speaking in tongues' is that strange phenomenon that names the ability to speak in languages one didn't know that one had mastery of. In German the word for dialect is *Mundart*, 'the manner of your mouth'. Unless we have some sense of how tongue and mouth interact in the bodily act of talking, we shall find it difficult to understand how children's spellings come to be as they are.

In the first section of this chapter I shall briefly say something about the way in which we make the sounds of speech. Perhaps the first thing to say is that our speech organs, so called, are not originally intended for speech at all. The vocal chords, which provide the vibration that makes vowels possible, and which give the 'tone' for 'intonation' – the melodic aspects of speech – are in fact a valve, which is designed to stop food from falling into your windpipe while you are breathing and eating. You can of course speak without using your vocal chords: it is called 'whispering'. When you whisper, the 'fullness', the 'body' of the sound of your voice is gone. Try it, to get a sense of what **voice** is, that part of speaking that depends on the vocal chords. The tongue itself has many functions, and aiding speech is not its original one: its main role is in digestion. Very many animals have tongues but do not use them to make (speech) sounds. In the evolutionary history of humans, the speech organs only relatively recently became adapted to speech; all of them – tongue, oral cavity, nasal cavity, lips, teeth, glottis, windpipe, vocal chords – had functions of a very different kind originally, and still have those functions now.

It is salutary and important to remind ourselves of this bodily aspect of speech. The speech organs are bits of our body that obey the same rules as do all other parts of our body. When we speak we use brain and muscles just as we do when we walk. For instance, I might put food into my mouth, chew it insufficiently (badly) and then swallow it, before it is fully chewed and really ready to be swallowed. Is that a right or a wrong, a 'correct' or 'incorrect', use of my digestive system? It is what I might do when I'm in a hurry; or perhaps it is what I have come to do by habit. As with all habitual, well-practised actions performed with our bodies, the more practised they are the more one thing moves into another, indistinguishably.

In much the same way, when I use these same organs to speak, I might not form each sound quite carefully, or not very well, but hurry from one to the next. One result of that will be that one sound slides into another: some sounds might be hardly pronounced at all, be hardly audible; and some might drop out entirely. If we treat speaking as the very ordinary use of a very ordinary set of muscles, then the kinds of things we do most naturally with our muscles will be seen to apply to speaking also. The more 'grooved' our actions are – say in playing a sport, in preparing food, in navigating traffic in a car or on foot – the less you will see the individual components of a complex action: one thing just slides smoothly into another.

6.2 Doing what comes naturally: losing the sounds of speech

Take a very simple example. A child (a 6-year-old) writes 'Rebekah has bumt her head' (6.0). Clearly, *bumt* is a spelling mistake. But before we rush to correct it, let us try to understand this mistake in terms of the two categories I mentioned earlier: that of **getting 'it' right**, and that of **getting 'it' correct**. We all agree that this spelling is incorrect: it should be *bumped* – though even as I spell this, I wonder whether there isn't in British English a possible version of spelling this as *bumpt*. Be that as it may, if you try to say this word it is very likely that you will actually say /bumt/. Indeed it is very difficult to say /bumpt/: that is, to say a clearly pronounced /p/ followed by a clearly pronounced /t/. If you try to do so, you are likely to produce something more like /bʌmpət/, where a weak vowel sound has appeared between the /p/ and the /t/.

What is the explanation? It lies in two things: in a combination of planning by the brain for producing the whole sound sequence, and in physiological constraints

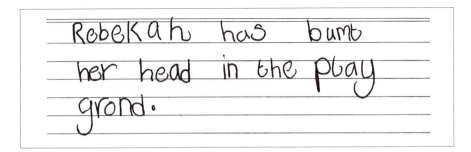

Figure 6.0

of the muscular movements of our speech organs, which prefer to do 'what comes most naturally'.

I'll try to do this explanation in slow motion.

First then, the planning by the brain. The brain has to plan the sounds we are going to say. It does this not 'one at a time', but as whole sequences of sounds. Second, these plans become instructions to the muscles that will carry out the movements of speech organs. Third, these movements actually get implemented in real time.

Let's consider what happens: the 'full' sound sequence for bumped is /b/, /ʌ/, /m/, /p/, /t/. But this sequence is pre-planned as a whole, not as individual sounds. As the muscles form the /b/, the brain has already sent instructions to the muscles to form the vowel /ʌ/. So even while the consonant /b/ is pronounced, the speech organs are getting ready – are preparing – for pronouncing the /ʌ/. As the /ʌ/ is pronounced the instructions for forming the /m/ are sent; as the /m/ is pronounced the instructions for the /p/ are under way.

For the pronunciation of the /m/ the vocal chords are vibrating, the lips are closed, and air is escaping through the nose (put the back of your hand under your nose while you're making an /m/ sound and you'll feel the air). The lip position is exactly the same as for the already prepared-for /p/, so no movement is necessary to get from /m/ to /p/; the flow of air through the nose has to be interrupted, otherwise no 'plosive' sound can be formed; but the final /t/ is already also planned for. The /t/ also requires that the flow of air is blocked, and then suddenly released: it, too, is a plosive consonant. But there isn't enough air to make two (ex)plosions. So what happens is this: the /m/ is formed, and pronounced. The lips are already making the gesture for the /p/, and the brain is already moving on to sending instructions to the speech organs to prepare for the /t/, with its major escape/explosion of air. In that process the /p/ is 'passed over' so to speak: it remains a mere 'gesture', and doesn't actually get pronounced. In the constant movement by the speech organs from one sound gliding into the next, the /p/ is just barely indicated but not ever pronounced.

This is no more or no less than with any series of moves by the body, whether in the execution of a golf swing, a backhand shot in tennis, a move in football, or a quick walk along a crowded shopping street. If you have to learn a tennis shot you will need to become conscious of a multiplicity of individual things, and of discrete positions: where your feet are and how they are positioned, the attitude of your body, the clasp of your hand, the angle of your wrist, your head movement, and the positions that the racket describes during the swing. For a practiced player all these merge into one continuous 'flow', and she or he will do things that are, strictly speaking, 'incorrect' in terms of a slow description of what should happen.

In summary, the consequence of all this is that the /p/ is not pronounced. The final -ed becomes pronounced as a voiceless /t/ because the preceding and unpronounced /p/ is also voiceless. The not-present, voiceless /p/ leaves as its only trace its voiceless quality, so to speak.

The child has heard the sounds accurately, and she has transcribed what she has heard precisely, with the means that she has available for doing so. But accurate transcription is not the same as correct spelling.

In Examples 6.1 and 6.2 there are a number of instances of a similar kind, in terms of the laws of sound production. All involve the elision of sounds: that is, instances where in normal/usual speech sounds disappear or **have** disappeared, have been elided, or have been assimilated to subsequent sounds.

In my estimation, about half of all children's 'misspellings' – getting the transcription right while getting the spelling wrong – are of this kind: eliding a sound that exists only in ideal (or idealized) pronunciations. In these instances, children are hearing acutely and transcribing precisely the facts of our everyday pronunciation, in which the speech organs and the brain combined do what we all do with all our grooved sequences of muscular actions – whether we're playing tennis or squash, driving a car, or preparing a meal. Such 'strange' pronunciations as *corpirtision* – competition, *prisas* (or *pritas*, produced by a similar process) – princess, *nax* – next, *trikig* – tricking, *wanuts* – walnuts, *patigs* – patterns, *climt* – climbed, *mostir* – monster, *ortirgriaf* – autograph, *mafs* – maths, and *orwise* – otherwise are all evidence of careful analysis and of attempts at precision in rendering the sounds of speech with the limited means of letters.

My point is not, of course, to leave it there and say that these young spellers are demonstrating enormous and intelligent effort (which they are), and that we need worry no further. Some of these misspellings are serious obstacles to communication – the reason usually advanced for the need to insist on conformity. Even those that are not are taken by others as departures from convention, and seen as signs of ignorance, of carelessness about rules, as a rejection of convention, as a lack of intelligence – and therefore they all have social consequences of a negative and often serious kind. This is quite sufficient reason to make me want to ensure that children should learn to spell. My question is this: Can we best achieve this aim of teaching spelling effectively if we understand fully the process of thought revealed in children's spelling? Predictably, my answer is: without that understanding we have a lesser chance of success. And: do we, in any case, get essential insights into how children act in their world, into their thoughts, their logics, from looking with open eyes at their actions? And equally clearly my answer is: we simply cannot afford to ignore this essential evidence.

My last set of examples (6.3) under this heading – 'loss of sounds – elision of sounds' brings a number of these together, combined with the issue that I shall discuss in a moment, that of the combination of the analysis of the stream of sound not just into the units of letters, but of words.

6.3 Working against nature: using the tools of culture to make meaning

In Examples 6.4 and 6.5 the problems encountered by the child, and the solutions adopted, all go in the opposite direction to that just discussed: not now the

Example 6.1

Hearing acutely, spelling incorrectly 1: lost consonants

(a) Nasalization: frad

The spelling of *friend* as *frad* is common for many children round about the age of 6 or 7. What is involved is the 'disappearance' of a sound, the /n/. The sounds that should be there are /frend/. The story of this disappearance goes as follows. As the vowel sound /e/ is made, the brain's planning is already shaping the posture of the speech organs for the /n/ and the /d/. Try saying /nd/ and you'll find that the tongue is in roughly the same position for both, just behind the small ridge inside the upper teeth (the **alveolar ridge**). What happens therefore is that quite often the brief /n/ in between /e/ and /d/ is not pronounced, or barely pronounced at all; instead, the /d/ becomes slightly nasalized, as a result of the nasal consonant /n/ (air escaping through the nasal chamber) that should have been there. That is, the sound quality of the /n/ that should have been there is transferred to the next sound.

The spelling may be a result of what the speaker said and how it was said (articulatory phonetics), and what the hearer heard and how she or he interpreted the sounds (acoustic phonetics).

(Continued on pages 200–201)

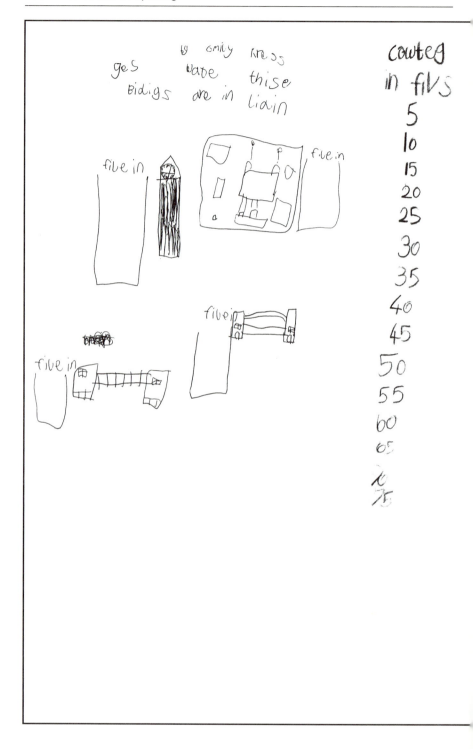

by emily kress

ges wabe thise Bidigs are in liain

cowteg in fiVs
5
lo
15
20
25
30
35
4o
45
50
55
bo
65
7o
75

five in

five in

five in

five in

Example 6.1 (continued)

(b) Elision and nasalization: bidigs

The missing /n/ sound in *building* is a result of the same process as in the example of *frad*: the nasal consonant is not pronounced, because the speech organs have already 'anticipated' the /g/. Normally, in the case of the combination of /n/ and /g/ the resulting sound is a /ng/, a fusion of nasal and plosive. The same effect as in *frad* and *bidigs* is produced when you have a heavy cold and your nasal chamber is blocked with mucus. Try saying *building* either while holding your nose, or while pretending that you have a cold.

The fate of the missing /l/ in *bidigs* is explained similarly to that of the missing /n/ in *frad*: the speech organs are anticipating the /d/, and on the way the /l/, which is made with the speech organs in a position very close to that of the /d/ but with a slight escape of air, becomes so brief as to disappear from notice. The sound quality of the /l/ becomes assimilated into the /d/.

Cowteg is just another instance of nasalization and assimilation. In both (a) and (b) the spelling is a result of what was said, and what was heard. Both spellings are actually evidence of acute hearing and precise phonetic analysis. The tongue moves from the diphthong /ou/ towards the already anticipated /t/, and on the way the tongue may make a brief 'gesture' at the /n/, which is not pronounced, however. The spellings also lead me to assume that the speller has tried these sounds out 'in her head', and has probably 'felt' how they were made in a silent articulation.

The process whereby a sound is 'assimilated' to a similar one close by is very common: it is 'natural'. The nasalization of many French words is the effect of precisely this process in the history of French.

1 egg
lose of Flawiv
10sc of shgav
and sime cocoa
and bek of 20 menis

Ths is a
eechaf a
house

Example 6.2

Hearing acutely, spelling incorrectly 2

In the recipe for the chocolate biscuits, there are two distinct instances of the elision of a /t/. Again the process whereby this happens, in *lose* (lots), is entirely natural. The explanation of this process has two components: one is the sudden release of air in the making of a plosive consonant (especially of a voiceless one such as /t/ or /p/ or /k/); the other is the fate of sounds at the end of words. The 'explosion' of air leads to a hissing noise as the air is released – a bit like letting air out of the valve of a car tyre, a kind of /ts/ sound. A /t/ therefore often ends in an *s*-like sound. In *lots* this is doubly so: the /t/, if it were fully pronounced, would finish with an *s*-like sound, and the word finishes with a (plural) /s/ in any case. The easiest solution in normal speech is simply to slide over the /t/, and leave it out entirely. Try saying *lots* (as in 'lots of time') with the /t/ pronounced, and with the /t/ gone. The former takes much more effort.

A very similar process happens with *minutes* /menis/: said quickly, the /t/ just disappears into the final /s/.

Pechaf [a] (a picture of) ('this is a Pechaf a house') is slightly more complicated, but the process is the same: the 'rule of least effort', as we might call it, applies here too. The word *picture* is rarely pronounced /pɪktjuə/, even by 'careful' speakers of Standard English.

More usually it is pronounced as /pɪktʃə/. In both these pronunciations there is a sequence of voiceless plosives /kt/ (as in the /pt/ of *bumped*), which nearly invariably leads to a pronunciation in which the first of the two is weakened, or elided altogether (- try saying the word with the /k/ and the /t/ clearly pronounced, and you will notice how 'unnatural' it is). That leaves /pɪtʃə/ (or /pikʃə/, both of which are common pronunciations. The first vowel, /ɪ/, is very likely to be 'reduced' to the vowel /ə/, the vowel of 'least effort'. That makes the pronunciation /pətʃə/ – which is exactly what the child has attempted with his use of *ch*.

The young speller had the additional problem of needing to decide how to segment the stream of sound into words: his analysis produced for him the sound-word *picture-of: pechaf*.

redog cone X

masbends X

Fasegame

WASGtheamamra W

gofe

belseg bema

Example 6.3

Turning the stream of sound into units of meaning

This example was produced by a $6\frac{1}{2}$-year-old in the context of a game of 'Fairs': it is a list of games available to those attending this particular fair: Reading corner, Mastermind, Face-game (?), What's the time Mr Wolf, Golf, Balancing beam.

Several of the examples are explained by the processes mentioned in Examples 6.1 and 6.2: *redeg cone* (reading corner) for instance, or *gofe* (golf) and *balseg bema* (balancing beam). In the latter, the /n/ before the /g/ is nasalized, and the syllable *an* (bala*n*cing) is assimilated into the preceding /l/. The *bema* is a matter both of visual/sequential ordering and, I think, of the local school's 'micro-dialect', in which an /ə/ or /a/ is frequently added to the end of words (as mentioned before) *o.k.a.*, *yesa* (usually spoken with hugely exaggerated rising then sharply falling intonation).

mastend (mastermind) is a case where the child has frequently heard the sound-word, but has no clear conception of what the word is and what it looks like. The rendering here is therefore more 'impressionistic', a kind of mnemonic for the word itself. The phonetic processes used by this child are, nevertheless, those discussed in all the preceding examples.

In both *mastend* and *balseg* a three-syllable word is shortened into a two-syllable word. This seems to me not so much a matter of 'dropping' or of 'missing out' a syllable, as a matter of 'compression' of the stream of sound of three syllables into two, in each case. The local (micro) dialect of the school is one in which you speak very fast indeed, so that individual, especially middle, syllables can easily get squashed up.

What this example illustrates is that the analysis of the stream of sound becomes harder for a speaker the less he or she knows the entity that is to be analysed.

the   gave choused

One   there was 3 Boys and
name is Girl and the girls
name is Leean and the Boys
and we   went to the /
I gave choued

Monday 17th   June

On sunday i went too the abbmit
and waen i Cam hoeum i wocht
a Vidyow from blok bist's then
it was iftr 9 a clok So then
i had too go to bed but i mist
my mum and dad but then iwas
owkay

Are langwidge / Englsh

Example 6.4

Striving to capture all the sounds

I have already briefly mentioned the *gave chaoued* example in the Introduction. This certainly posed a considerable puzzle for a colleague and myself; we simply didn't know what this 12-year-old was trying to spell. The easy way out here, as so often, would have been to give up and assume that this was, simply, carelessly scribbled nonsense. But the explanation of this spelling lies in a combination of factors: the sounds of the dialect that this (12-year-old) child hears, and which he himself may be speaking, and the painstaking attempt at making sense of that sound.

Gave (grave: /greɪv/) is quickly explained: the /r/ is a sound that can easily be weakened or can disappear altogether in the tongue's movement from the dipthong /eɪ/ to the voiced consonant /v/. *Chaoued* is a lot more complicated. The *y* in *yard* is usually pronounced as a semi-vowel. Semi-vowels, as their name suggests, are hybrids, which exist between vowels (no obstruction to the flow of air) and consonants (some obstruction to the flow of air); and they can become more vowel-like or more consonant-like in pronunciation. If you say 'yacht' you are likely to hear a kind of friction noise as you pronounce the y: that is the result of the slight resistance offered to the air as it moves between the tongue and the palate; it is the sound /j/. Some speakers in some dialects make that friction noise much more intense, nearly into a /ʃ/ as in *shard*. That is what this speller seems to have heard, or to have imagined, as he was spelling the word. The *aoue* has an explanation that relates to the initial semi-vowel *y*, /j/, and to the fact that the vowel in *yard* is long, as most *ar* combinations tend to be (*far, tar, target*, etc.). The *ar* is followed by a voiced vowel /d/, so the vocal chords are vibrating continuously throughout the pronunciation of *yard*. This tends to turn the single vowel /a:/ into quite a long sound; and the longer a vowel sound is, the more likely it is to 'wobble', to 'waver', to turn into something more like a sequence of slightly different vowels, like a diphthong or even a triphthong. This is what this speller heard, or imagined he heard.

If we accept this explanation we have a completely new image of this child and of his attempts at spelling. No longer is he the careless incompetent: he is revealed as a child who really tries, who has acute hearing, and a precision of rendering sounds that is astonishing.

Hoeum (written by a 6-year-old) has exactly the same explanation: the child strives to record the diphthong or triphthong /ou/ precisely, she thinks (correctly) that she has heard an /e/-like sound between the /o/ and the /u/, and she records it in her spelling.

(Continued on pages 208–209)

Example 6.4 (continued)

When a 6-year-old writes *hoeum* we are likely to say that this child has not yet learned to spell properly – perhaps she got herself confused by the final *e* in *home*; when a 12-year old writes *chaoued* we are less tolerant – this child **should** know how to spell by this stage. We are less ready to 'make allowances', to find a reason, an excuse or even an explanation. Of course, the latter is precisely what this child needs if we are ever to help him.

The last few examples – *langwidge*, *panadoals (panadols)*, *stapills (staples)* and *dezinening* (designing) – are explained by the same logic, the logic of wishing to make sure all the sounds are there, precisely. I have included them simply to give some further examples.

Frogs born.   James

When Frogs are born there called
frogs born and there in littel rond bits of
jelly so they coñt do nofing.

Tadpolc + frog   5/2/97
I already knew that frog's have
Baby's.   I have leafnt tath tadpole
come at of frog's sporn. ✓
I allso loarñt that thay they Brev uder
water. hawever the mose
interesting thing was that
the tadfod are the blak
spoes

Example 6.5

Dialect: what you hear is what you get

Two examples that I discussed in Chapter 2 can serve to make the main point here. In the 'Frog's born' example the young speller wrote *there in littel rond bits of jelly so they con't do nofing. Nofing* is clearly (North) London dialect; it is what the child hears, and what he says. *Littel* (rather than *little*) may also be 'fostered' by his dialect; in North London dialect there is often a clear /e/ between the /t/ and the final /l/ of /lɪtel/.

The speller who wrote *I allso learnt that thay Brev uda water* hears the same dialect, and I feel certain that this accounts for her *brev* (breathe); *uda* (under) is an instance of the loss of the sound /n/ before the /d/, with the consequent slight 'nasalization' of the /d/. She is author of *a bush* (see example 6.7), in which she writes *and sime win cims and pikes it up and frows it away:* here, too, the *frows* is what she hears. She is also the speller of *Mafs* (Maths), an entirely accurate transcription of her peer group's pronunciation. Her parents (sometimes) make a point of suggesting the alternative *th* /θ/ form. Clearly the peer group rules at this stage.

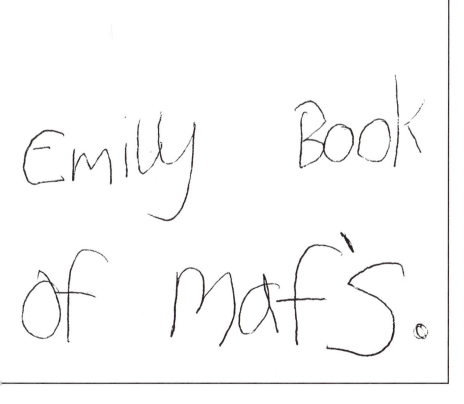

elision of sounds, but an attempt on the child's part to make sure that all the sounds that he or she feels ought to be there are actually represented.

The question of what dialect of English the child hears and speaks is clearly a crucial one: if spelling is in part a transliteration of sound into letters, then in a very real sense the child must rely on what she or he hears. In Example 6.4, I make some speculations about that. In Example 6.5, I want to show some quite specific instances of this.

In 6.4 and 6.5, the examples show children trying to capture precisely the sound quality of the words they were spelling. In the following examples they are attempting to determine, to fix, how the word is to be sounded – they are striving very hard to achieve a specific sound effect. I have already discussed this in Chapter 3, in Example 3.16. Here I want to discuss two further examples to demonstrate the precision with which children accomplish this task.

6.4 Making sure the sound is beautiful: spelling for aesthetic effect

Example 6.8 mimics, in its graphic display, the object that it is describing, a whale. Here, just as in 6.7, but perhaps even more intensely, the speller aims for a specific sound shape to match the intense sentiments of her poem.

6.5 Spelling to mean

I want to turn now to the question of the sound of the larger meaning-units, the words and phrases used in writing. I have discussed this matter earlier, but as it is so intricately caught up with the question of the sound of language it may be worth taking up once more.

In Example 6.10, *My one dided*, I suggest that spelling is, at one level, influenced not so much by what one actually hears, or by what one actually sees, but by what one thinks one knows. The speller of *dided* knows, at this point, that you form the past tense of English verbs by putting *-ed* on the end of the verb. This is 'knowledge' produced by the generalizing, abstracting function of the brain: it is not knowledge derived from the world, so to speak – whereas the speller of *beable* in Example 6.10 did spell what she heard, what came from the world. The speller of *Paklich*, in Example 6.11, also knows something, but this is not knowledge that comes from the world, as in *beable*, nor is it quite the result of the generalizing and abstracting work of the brain as in *dided*, where the young speller had produced a grammatical rule for himself. *Paklich* is the result of a 'mishearing': the child heard a sound sequence, and superimposed on it a shape that seemed plausible in terms of the syllabic and phonological rules of her language.

a   bush

the bush   gose   this way
and that intit a life fals
off and sime win cims
and Pikes it up and fraes it away

the end

Example 6.6

Writing the 'score' for precise pronunciation

The writer here uses her graphic 'beautiful writing' style – as in other examples already discussed (i.e. in 3.14, or in 3.16). But I want to draw attention here particularly to the spelling of words such as *intil, fols* (falls), *sime win cims* (some one comes), *pikes* (picks). In other instances of her spelling at the same time, this speller uses quite 'normal' spelling for words such as *until, someone*. It seems that here she is absolutely determined to aim for and achieve a specific style of delivery – pursed lips, finely articulated sound – a quite specific holding of the verbal gestural apparatus, and a specific sound – not the dull, flat /ʌ / of *someone* /sʌmʌn/, *come* (cʌm), etc. She seems to be determined to aim for a particular vowel quality. For a word like *until*, the letter that might lead to achieving it is the high short vowel /ɪ/– precise, sharp,clearly articulated; hence *intil*. I feel that the same is the case with the /o/ of *fols, sime win*, and all the other spellings. This is spelling that aims to ensure precision in performance of the sound that is to be produced in speaking the poem.

'Normalized spelling'
a bush
the bush goes this way and that
until a leaf falls off
and someone comes
and picks it up
and throws it away

the end

Example 6.7

Spelling rhythmic features and melodies of sound

Several of the features discussed in Example 6.6 and elsewhere are evident here, in this visual and aural poem about whales. One feature that struck me in particular is the seeming experimentation with the spelling of whale: *wayos, weyos, weyols, wayols.* In its normal pronunciation *whale* is a monosyllabic word; here, in all four instances, it has two syllables. This has been achieved through spelling and, I think, for rhythmic effect. Of course, the rhythmic effect also has semantic consequences: a double-syllable word is poetically more 'weighty'; it has more 'gravity' than a single syllable word.

The poem begins and ends with the word spelled with an *l*: here, as in examples I discussed earlier, the motivation seems to be to achieve a quite specific sound effect: rounded, fuller, weightier.

the wayols swim in the depa blow see
and wee ole say: save thos wayos
save thes weyos,
ow ples, ow ples
Jest save those weyols.

To me, the abiding impression here is of spelling used in the service of poetic effect, of scansion, in the service of rhythm. Certainly it is incorrect spelling; but, poetically, it is precise and effective.

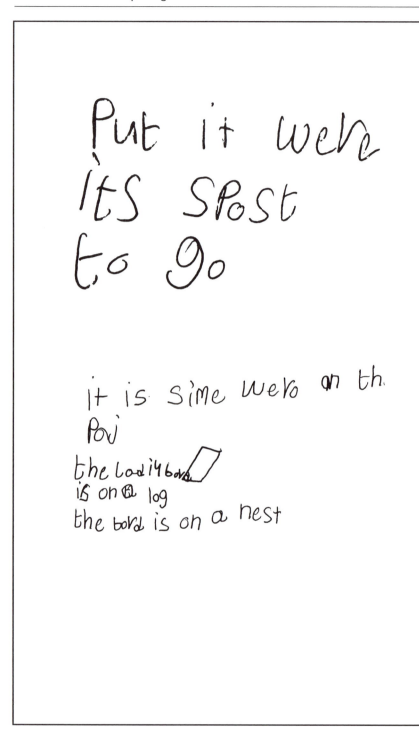

Put it wehe
Its Spost
to go

it is sime wero an th.
Pou
the Lodi4bord
is on a log
the bord is on a nest

Example 6.8

The meaning of units of sound

The examples here are relatively straightforward, though they do illustrate the issue well enough. Apart from the fact that this 6-year old does not know how to spell *where*, her spelling indicates the wobbly sense that she has of words: *its spost* tends to suggest, the way it is written here, a kind of structure such as *its nest, its home*, although the infinitive *to go*, that follows, rules that out as a possibility, in adult language at any rate. What the example shows is that without a sense of the grammatical structure of the stream of sound it is difficult or impossible to spell. However, if we take that insight seriously, then our conception of spelling has moved a very long way, from the straightforward one of 'transliteration of sound into letters', or from 'the correct reproduction of the graphic units of written language'.

Much the same can be said of the second example: although the sense here is clear, the knowledge of words and their component elements is shaky. These spellings are based on having heard these words, not on having seen them: they are informed guesses in terms of the framings of the words and in terms of their grammatical function. Again, if we take this insight seriously, we see that spelling rests on a prior knowledge of language as a visual phenomenon, a knowledge of the look of words.

What is clear from these is that spelling from sound alone is not enough. Spelling is deeply embedded in the shape, the *look* of words and of their grammar. And all of these depend on a prior sense about their meaning. But a slogan such as 'without meaning, no spelling' has taken us a long way from notions of spelling as routines of transliteration.

hers More coke a ray book

the plese
are out
and in wachrose worche today
ther was not much bere

thes   a coo a roybook in the nwsepapor
today . Monday is a bisyday
mums and dads are rosheg to wrko

today
is the frst
of Sctabor
its my
bortnday

Example 6.9

Spelling to mean 1: grammar as an essential support

On the day this 6-year-old produced these two texts, the *Observer* newspaper had featured some recipes, and she and her mother had talked about these before going off to Waitrose, a local supermarket.

My attention was caught by the child's experimentation in trying to make sense of the sound sequence *cookery book*. The transliteration of the sound of both *coo a reybook* and *coke a rey book* (as of words such as *rosheg* – rushing, *wachrose* – Waitrose) can be explained by the earlier examples – the disappearance of the *k* in the one case, the letter *a* used to transcribe the vowel of *cookery*, etc. But it is equally clear that a sense of the sound shape alone is simply not enough: the child needs the visual sense of the word **and** a clear sense of the grammar in which the word appears. Here most of the experimentation is with grammar/syntax: *a* (article), *coo* (adjective?), *a* (article), *reybook* (noun), *yore* (pronoun), *coke* (verb?), *a* (article), *rey* (adjective), *book* (noun).

Dear   mum
would i beabel   to pull

Week 3

Root 5 mm

26m
becôuse my
one dided.

Example 6.10

Spelling to mean 2: without grammar no meaning; without meaning no hope of spelling correctly

Here are two more examples of the child's need for understanding of what meaning is at issue, a sense of lexis, a sense of words as visual, and a sense of grammar, in order to be able to spell. In ... *would I beable to pul* ..., *beable* is treated by the child as a single word – a verb – (analogous to ... *would I want to borrow your car* ...) which is used 'correctly' in relation to a particular syntactic structure, an interrogative: the declarative form would be *I would be able to pul*.

In *My one dided* the problem lies not just in the spelling. This child is at a point where he is trying out the grammar of irregular and regular verbs: here the issue is the formation of the past tense. He has heard *died* (/daid/) but is not aware of its written form. He is speculating here on what the written form should/would look like, and he comes up with this solution. At the same time he is struggling with the quite separate and general issue of the past tense forms of verbs, at a stage when he 'overgeneralizes' and produces forms such as *hit – hitted*. What he is spelling is influenced as much by what he 'knows' abstractly and generally about grammar, as by what he thinks he hears.

Pak Lich   Rebe kah ✓

Iona ✓ EMilY✓   LoLa ✗

Misha ✗

Example 6.11

'Mishearing'? or putting a shape on the world

With this example I want to raise, as a last point, the question whether 'misspelling' is ever the result of error simply and straightforwardly, or whether there is – in my schema at any rate – no such thing as an error.

Here the child has written the names of several of her school mates as part of a game of playing 'school': she is calling the roll. I have maintained that children are accurate recorders of their world – which in the case of spelling is of the world of speech-sound and of the world of the visual. But surely Paklich is clearly a 'mishearing', and therefore a misspelling based on a mistake about representing the world?

My answer is that all hearing (as indeed all perception) is always the result of the work of interpretation, and that interpretation is based on the knowledge with which we approach the world. That knowledge shapes our perception – whether in seeing or in hearing – and it is constantly modified in the process of engaging with the world. Here the child may **not** have been certain about what she has heard, but what she is certain about is that she wants to have a clear sense of the visible shape, the look of what she needs to have recorded on her roll.

I do think that children make 'errors', and can be and are careless. I also think that if we take this last assumption as the basis of our approach to their spelling, we have provided ourselves with an overwhelming alibi that rules out careful looking before we even start.

In   the   artgalivey.
there   are   Powims.
there   are   droring.
there   are   mafs.
there are Patigs.
and   a   tonk abawt it and a sprise
and   sim e modobs

In the artgallery
there are poems.
there are drawings.
there are maps.
there are paintings.
and a talk about it and a surprise
and some models.

Example 6.12

In the 'artgalirey'

I want to conclude with another instance of highly deliberate spelling, in the dimensions of visual aesthetics, of the aesthetics of sound, and in the dimension of the overall shaping of the text. The transliterations of sound – *powims, droring, mafs, tork*, etc. – are entirely in line with the explanations I have given before: a mixture of striving for accuracy and wishing to 'fix', to determine the sound-shape of the text as it is to be read. It is written in this speller's 'beautiful' or 'heightened' writing style and, as I have said, that for me is also a spelling of meaning. The layout on the page indicates a concern for the spelling of the shape of the text as visual object.

A brief glossary of terms

consonant A speech sound made with some obstruction to the air as it passes from the lungs through the vocal organs. The obstruction may be complete and end in a sudden expulsion of air (plosive consonants: /p/, /b/, /t/, /d/, /k/, /g/); or it may be partial, allowing continued passage of the air, but with friction (/f/, /s/, etc.); or there may be some obstruction of a different kind (/l/, /r/). Consonants may be made with vocal chords vibrating (voiced consonants: /b/, /m/); or not vibrating (voiceless consonants: /p/, /f/)

grammar The term **grammar** is used to describe the regularities of language at the level of **words** and **sentences**. It comprises the study of (a) words (as meaningful elements) – morphology – and of their components – **morphemes**; and (b) the combination of words (as formal elements – 'the parts of speech') into the larger units of phrases, clauses and sentences – the study of **syntax**.

lexis The study of the smallest complete meaning-units. These are often, or most usually, words. But often several words make up one **lexeme**: for instance, in English the verb *run up* as in 'He ran up a huge hill'; or the fusions of words as in *railway station*, which are single units of meaning, even though they have not (yet) become fully fused as in *airport*.

linguistics The discipline that has been developed in Western cultures to study language.

morphemes This term is used to show that in languages such as English the **word** is not the smallest unit of meaning; the morpheme is. In a word such as *hunted* there are two morphemes: the lexical stem *hunt*, which expresses the dictionary meaning, so to speak, and the morpheme *-ed*, which expresses the grammatical meaning, that of past tense. In a word such as *unusually* there are three morphemes: the lexical stem *usual*, the negative prefix *un-*, and the suffix *-ly*, which indicates the grammatical function of this word (as 'part of speech') as an adverb.

morphology   The study of morphemes.

phoneme   The 'stream' of speech consists of identifiable sounds, the **phonemes**. They are recognizable to speakers of a language as being instances of a type. This roundabout definition is necessary because the type
never exists in a pure, ideal form, but always in a constantly varying appearance. The /t/ of *tower* is a differently sounding /t/ from that in 'but you said
. . .' These contextual variants of phonemes are called **allophones**: they
have no graphic correspondences in English (though they do in some other
alphabetic writing systems, to some extent, such as that of Arabic for
instance).

   Until we are fully competent 'in' a language we are likely to be unclear
about what these ideal types are. This leads to problems for children in their
spelling: they are more likely to try to spell what they actually hear, than to
try to spell the ideal types, which they may not be fully aware of.

   As far as spelling is concerned, in alphabetic languages there is an assumption that by and large phonemes are represented by letters, based on an
implicit assumption that in an ideal world letters are the graphic representations of phonemes.

phonetics   The study of the physical characteristics of the speech-sounds of
human languages. Articulatory phonetics deals with speech production: that
is, how all the speech organs act together to make speech sounds. Acoustic
phonetics deals with speech reception: that is, how the ear receives and – to
some extent – the brain processes the sounds of speech. Both of these offer
important insights into the problems of spelling encountered by those learning to spell.

phonology   The study of the sound-systems of languages.

semiotics   The discipline that studies the variety of means used in human
cultures to make meaning. It encompasses the study of language, of
images, of gesture, as some of many modes for representation and
communication.

semi-vowels   Semi-vowels have both vowel-like and consonant-like characteristics: they are produced with the vocal chords vibrating, and the obstruction
offered to the air is so slight that there is a vowel-like quality to them; at the
same time there is obstruction, which makes them consonant-like. Speakers
(and dialects) differ in the degree to which they make semi-vowels more vowel-
like or more consonant-like. The initial sound as in *yacht* is a semi-vowel; so
is the initial sound as in Scottish *where*.

   In the structure of syllables, semi-vowels act as though they were
consonants. Because of their somewhat indeterminate sound characteristics,

and their function in syllables, semi-vowels present particular problems to children in their spelling.

spelling   Dictionary definitions of 'spelling' tend to focus on the correct representation of words by means of sequences of letters. In practice, and in the usage of anglophone societies, spelling refers as much – or more – explicitly or implicitly to the relation between speech-sounds and their graphic representation by letters. This may be a consequence of the particularly complex mismatch between sound sequences and letter sequences in English, a result of the history of the English language, a history of the alphabet and the history of scribal practices.

In monolingual societies there has been, and persists, a notion that a language is spelled with one spelling system. In pluri-lingual societies (in India, for instance), but also in a monolingual one such as Japan, it is entirely taken for granted that a language may be spelled with any one of a number of spelling systems, and that the spelling systems may intermingle, for the achievement of particular effects – as in poetry or in advertising for instance.

syllables   Syllables are the actual 'building blocks' of the sound-sequences of a language such as English. A syllable always consists of a vowel, and usually has consonants – one or more – associated with the vowel. The vowel is therefore the essential and criterial element. Typical syllable structures in English are:

> vowel – v: *a*
> consonant + vowel – cv: *to*
> consonant + vowel + consonant – cvc: *put*
> consonant + consonant + vowel + consonant + consonant – ccvcc: *brisk*
> consonant + dipthong – cvv: *fire* etc.

Languages have permissible and impermissible syllable structures. In English *stroppy* is possible, but *postr* is not. This fact has a bearing on the spelling of loanwords, where the permissible structures from one language are brought into another language where they may not be permissible.

syntax   The combination of the grammatical elements into the elements that make up sentences and below-sentence-level units, such as **phrases** and **clauses**.

text   When we speak or write, it is on particular social occasions, and in doing so we produce extended pieces of language: texts. Despite a commonsense view, we do not communicate in words or sentences, but in texts. Words and sentences are elements of text. Text is important for spelling, because it is in the environment of a text (and of its own wider social and material environment) that children meet the units that they have to spell. They need and take information from text (and from its environments), as from sentences, to make decisions about meaning-shape, the sound-shape or the look of the entitities they have to spell.

vowels   Vowels are speech sounds made with the vocal chords vibrating, and no obstruction offered by the speech organs to the air as it passes from lungs through the vocal tract.

word   Words seem simple things to define, but they lead a tricky life. It is helpful to think of words in three ways: as a unit of sound or of graphic form; as a unit of meaning; and as a unit with a grammatical role. Words always have all three characteristics at the same time. The word *hunt* has a sound-shape when spoken, and a graphic shape when written; it 'means' something – the kind of definition we look for in a dictionary; and it always has a grammatical role as a 'part of speech' – it will either be a verb, or it will be a noun. Dictionaries tend to treat *hunt*-as-verb as a distinct word, separate from *hunt*-as-noun.

Bibliography

Albrow, K.H. (1972) *The English Writing System*, London: Longman.

Arnheim, R. (1969) *Visual Thinking*, Los Angeles: University of California Press.

Barrs, M. (1988) 'Maps of play,' in M. Meek and C. Mills (eds) *Language and Literacy in the Primary School*, Lewes: Falmer Press.

Barton, D. and Hamilton, M. (1997) *Local Literacies*, London: Routledge.

Bissex, G. (1980) *GNYS AT WRK: A Child Learns to Read and Write*, Cambridge, MA: Harvard University Press.

Bruner, J. (1990) *Acts of Meaning*, Cambridge, MA: Harvard University Press.

Bruner, J. (1996) 'Frames for thinking: ways of making meaning,' in D. Olson and N. Torrance (eds) *Modes of Thought: Explanations in Culture and Cognition*, Cambridge: Cambridge University Press.

Bryant, P.E. and Bradley, L. (1985) *Children's Reading Problems*, Oxford: Blackwell.

Corson, D. (1985) *The Lexical Bar*, Oxford: Pergamon Press.

Clark, R. and Ivanic, R. (1997) *The Politics of Writing*, London: Routledge.

Fairclough, N. (1989) *Language and Power*, London: Longman.

Ferreiro, E. and Teberosky, A. (1997) *Literacy Before Schooling*, London: Heinemann.

Frith, U. (1980) *Cognitive Processes in Spelling*, New York: Academic Press.

Gardner, H. (1993) *Frames of Mind: The Theory of Multiple Intelligence*, London: Harper Collins.

Gee, J. (1990) *Social Linguistics and Literacies: Ideology in Discourse*, Lewes: The Falmer Press.

Gee, J. (1992) *The Social Mind: Language, Ideology, and Social Practice*, London: Bergin & Garvey.

Gee, J., Hull, G. and Lankshear, C. (1996) *The New Work Order: Behind the language of the new capitalism*, Boulder, CO: Westview.

Gimson, A.C. (1962) *An Introduction to the Pronunciation of English*, London: Edward Arnold.

Goodman, K. (1994) *Phonic Phacts*, Richmond Hill: Ontario Scholastic, Canada, Ltd.

Goswani, U. and Bryant, P. (1990) *Phonological Skills and Learning to Read*, Hove: Lawrence Erlbaum.

Hall, N. (1987) *The Emergence of Literacy*, London: Hodder & Stoughton.

Hall, N. (1992) *Writing with Reason*, London: Hodder & Stoughton

Halliday, M.A.K. (1975) *Learning How to Mean*, London: Edward Arnold.

Harris, R. (1991) *The Origins of Writing*, London: Duckworth.

Hodge, R.I.V. and Kress, G.R. (1988) *Social Semiotics*, Cambridge: Polity Press.

Kamler, B. and Killorr, G. (1983) 'Looking at what children can do; in B.M. Kroll and G. Wells (eds) *Explorations in the Development of Writing*, London: John Wiley.

Kress, G.R. (1993) *Learning to Write*, London: Routledge.

Kress, G.R. (1995) *Writing the Future: English and the Making of a Culture of Innovation*, Sheffield: NATE.

Kress, G.R. (1997) *Before Writing: Rethinking the Paths to Literacy*, London: Routledge.

Kress, G.R. and van Leeuwen, T. (1996) *Reading Images: The Grammar of Visual Design*, London: Routledge.

Lankshear, C. and Gee, J. P. (1997) *Changing Literacies*, Buckingham: Open University Press.

Leith, R. (1983) *A Social History of English*, London: Routledge & Kegan Paul.

Olson, D.R. (1994) *The World on Paper: The Conceptual and Cognitive Implications of Reading and Writing*, Cambridge: Cambridge University Press.

Pahl, K. (1999) *Transformations: Meaning Making in Nursery Education*, London: Trentham Books.

Piaget, J. (1959) *The Language and Thought of the Child* (translated M. Gabain and R. Gabain), London: Routledge & Kegan Paul.

Rampton, B. (1996) *Crossings*, London: Longman.

Read, C. (1986) *Children's Creative Spelling*, London: Routledge & Kegan Paul.

Riley, J. (1996) *The Teaching of Reading: The Development of Literacy in the Early Years of School*, London: Paul Chapman.

Sacks, O. (1991) *Seeing Voices*, London: Macmillan.

Saussure, F. de (1974) *Course in General Linguistics*, London: Peter Owen.

Sebba, M. (1994) *London Jamaican*, London: Longman.

Skeat, W.W. (1963) *An Etymological Dictionary of the English Language*, Oxford: Oxford University Press.

Stubbs, M. (1980) *Language and Literacy*, London: Routledge & Kegan Paul.

Stubbs, M. (1986) *Educational Linguistics*, Oxford: Blackwell.

Sulzby, E. (1986) 'Writing and reading organization', in W. Teale and E. Sulzby (eds) *Emergent Literacy: Writing and Reading*, Norwood, NJ: Ablex.

Sulzby, E. (1992) 'Research directions: transitions from emergent to conventional writing,' *Language Arts*, 69: 291–7.

Temple, C., Nathan, R., Burns, N. and Temple, F. (1988) *The Beginnings of Writing*, New York: Allyn and Bacon.

Vygotsky, L.S. (1978) *Mind in Society: The Development of Higher Psychological Processes*. Cambridge, MA: Harvard University Press.

Vygotsky, L.S. (1986) *Thought and Language*, Cambridge, MA: Harvard University Press.

van Leeuwen, T. (1999) *The Semiotics of Sound*, London: Macmillan.

Wells, G. (1987) *The Meaning Makers: Children Learning Language and Using Language to Learn*, London: Hodder & Stoughton.

Wertsch, J.V. (1991) *Voices of the Mind: A Sociocultural Approach to Mediated Action*, Hemel Hempstead: Harvester Wheatsheaf.

Index